SOCCER

SOCCER
THE PLAYER'S HANDBOOK

M. B. ROBERTS
PHOTOGRAPHS BY RONALD C. MODRA

STERLING

New York / London
www.sterlingpublishing.com

STERLING and the distinctive Sterling logo are registered trademarks
of Sterling Publishing Co., Inc.

Library of Congress Cataloging-in-Publication Data

Roberts, M. B. (Mary Beth)
  Soccer : the player's handbook / M.B. Roberts ; photographs by
Ronald C. Modra.
     p. cm.
  Includes bibliographical references and index.
  ISBN 978-1-4027-5872-0 (pb-trade pbk. : alk. paper)
1. Soccer—Handbooks, manuals, etc. I. Modra, Ronald C. pht II.
Title.

  GV943.R55 2010
  796.334—dc22

                  2009013682

10   9   8   7   6   5   4   3   2   1

Published by Sterling Publishing Co., Inc.
387 Park Avenue South, New York, NY 10016
Text © 2010 by M. B. Roberts
Photos © 2010 by Ronald C. Modra
Distributed in Canada by Sterling Publishing
c/o Canadian Manda Group, 165 Dufferin Street
Toronto, Ontario, Canada M6K 3H6
Distributed in the United Kingdom by GMC Distribution Services
Castle Place, 166 High Street, Lewes, East Sussex, England BN7 1XU
Distributed in Australia by Capricorn Link (Australia) Pty. Ltd.
P.O. Box 704, Windsor, NSW 2756, Australia

Photography by Ronald C. Modra

Sterling ISBN 978-1-4027-5872-0

For information about custom editions, special sales, and premium
and corporate purchases, please contact Sterling Special Sales
Department at 800-805-5489 or specialsales@sterlingpublishing.com.

CONTENTS

FOREWORD

Soccer is the most popular sport in the world. All over the globe, people are attached to this game in deep and passionate cultural ways.

In the United States, even though the professional game hasn't been completely embraced by most sports fans, soccer is in the mainstream. Millions of kids are playing soccer every weekend all over the country. People love playing the sport, they love being involved in the sport, and the game gives much to them. That's why the soccer community is growing at such a phenomenal rate.

Today, soccer is front and center in the lives of many families. Just look in the media. Ads on TV and in magazines show soccer moms loading their kids in the car to go to soccer practice. It's part of the culture, whether you were born here or you moved here from another country and brought your love and knowledge of soccer with you. There is a truly vibrant soccer scene out there. But it took us a while to get here.

In the late sixties, high-school soccer players were still in the minority, but I grew up in Westport, Connecticut, where soccer was a big part of the community. Staples High School, where I played varsity soccer, was legendary for winning annual state championships and sending dozens of players to top soccer colleges and later to the North American Soccer League (NASL).

With the establishment of the NASL, new hope emerged for the growth of soccer here in America. For me in 1974, a senior on the soccer team at the University of Pennsylvania, this was incredibly exciting because I now had the opportunity to play pro soccer. I played for the Miami Toros for three years and in 1976 even battled against Pele at Yankee Stadium.

Even though the NASL struggled and eventually disbanded in 1984, the spark that ignited a new era in the development of soccer in the United States was lit. As I moved on to become a high-school coach and later a college coach, I watched something incredible happen. Youth clubs were popping up everywhere. Soon, there wasn't a field in America where kids weren't playing soccer on Saturdays and Sundays.

The NASL was the engine behind this initial growth.

But of course there are many reasons for the explosion of the youth game in this country. First, soccer offers lots of opportunities for children to run, jump, twist, create, and express, matching perfectly the desires of every six-year-old. While "real" soccer requires large fields, youth soccer can thrive on smaller patches of grass that turn baseball outfields into hives of goal-scoring celebrations. Soccer does not require a lot of equipment, and it provides lots of exercise in a safe environment. And perhaps most importantly of all, it's gender-neutral and encourages the participation of both sexes. The enactment of Title IX was a huge development for sports in America, and soccer was often the perfect solution to parity for boys and girls in sports. The timing was right.

Playing sports—any sport—offers the opportunity for players to develop qualities that will help them as they strive for excellence in their lives. Perseverance. Commitment. Leadership. But soccer may be one of the best sports where an individual can truly grow and develop. This is a sport that demands its players take on a lot of responsibility for what happens in the game. There are no time-outs. The game runs uninterrupted. Much responsibility for team success and excellence rests with each individual player.

Even so, it's difficult to score a goal. It requires everyone working together. That's what sets our game apart. It's the ultimate team sport. Perhaps the most important thing to remember is that kids love to play this game because it is so free-flowing and fosters much creativity and expression. During the match itself, coaches actually have very little influence on the players. It's important to let kids experience the joy and heartbreak that comes when they are responsible for the outcome of the game. Coaches (and parents!) need to resist the urge to impose too much structure during practice and to give too many instructions during the game.

Kids are inherently creative. They want to be active and expressive. They want to enjoy and revel in their time on the field. Our job is to make sure that when our coaching experience is over, they still have that same passion. Let's make sure that when they leave our team and they move on to the next level, their love of the game is flourishing.

At the National Soccer Hall of Fame and Museum, our mission is to energize participation, inspire excellence, and celebrate achievement in the world's most popular sport. We're hopeful that the experiences we facilitate compel people to imagine and engage in a lifetime of distinction. Soccer provides a wonderful platform to emphasize those values and qualities that are so important to a vibrant and nurturing community. I am hopeful that this wonderful book will inspire you to create soccer experiences that contribute to the development of your players and your community. Now there's a goal!

Stephen H. Baumann
President
National Soccer Hall of Fame and Museum

Acknowledgments

This book could not have happened without the expertise and enthusiasm of Cindy and Doug Taylor and their awesome and knowledgeable soccer-playing sons, Shaun and Ryan. Thanks for all the ideas, for fact-checking, and for being our safety net. A special thank-you to Coach Trip Ellis for organizing and leading the demonstrations performed by FC Richmond players and for contributing many valuable resources for this book.

Thanks to all the players (and prodding parents) who contributed quotes for the book, especially Tori Leech, the Gipsons of Ijamsville, the young King sisters in Brazil, and the Baumhower brood in Alabama.

Thank you to Nick Stanczyk for demonstrating weight training moves and to James Cordell for supervising the session at Mariner's Hospital in Tavernier, Florida. Thanks also to U.S. Men's National Team fitness coach Pierre Barrieu for training tips and to Erika Barahona, Juan Matheus, and Dave Hillend for contributing to the referee section.

Thank you also to Jack Huckel and Steve Baumann at the National Soccer Hall of Fame, to Neil Buethe and John Hackworth at U.S. Soccer, and to Jim Thompson at The Positive Coaching Alliance for permission to quote from his books and Web site.

Thanks also to FIFA (Fédération Internationale de Football Association) for the generous permission to quote from the rules, also known as The Laws of the Game. (Note: Direct quotes are printed in italics.)

—M.B. Roberts

—Ron Modra

1: KICKOFF

The Ins and Outs of the Global Game

Soccer—or "football," as it is called in most parts of the world—is the most popular game on the planet. There's just something about soccer, which over the years has earned nicknames including the Beautiful Game, the Simplest Game, the World's Game, and the People's Game. The international governing body, the Fédération Internationale de Football Association (FIFA), boasts more countries among its membership than the United Nations. No other sport has so many passionate players and fans.

THE WORLD'S GAME

People have been playing soccer, or games that loosely resemble soccer, for thousands of years. Things became official in 1863 when a group of players and managers from English public schools got together in London and wrote a set of rules for the sport. Of course, they called it "football," which is how most of the world refers to it. But another game by that name was developing in the United States around the same time, so Americans called their version of the sport "soccer"—a slang abbreviation for Association Football, England's soccer league.

Despite the fact that soccer dominates just about every park and youth field in the United States, it's still a growing, developing sport in America. Internationally, it's a different story. Soccer is played from the United Arab Emirates to the former Soviet Republic of Moldova. They play in London, Nairobi, Beijing, and, of course, St. Louis and Savannah.

In Brazil, soccer is everywhere. Kids dribble and pass the ball to each other while waiting for the school bus. Entire cities shut down during big tournaments, and no one expects to do business during the World Cup.

Soccer passions run high in other parts of the world as well. In 1978, a German nun was arrested when she

American kids are ready to play.

attempted to strangle a man cheering for Austria during its World Cup victory over West Germany. In Italy, Parliament has been shut down over an argument about soccer. In London, families have been divided over alliances to rival clubs. The same holds true throughout South America, Europe, Asia, and Africa.

So why is soccer so beloved?

Part of the reason is the egalitarian nature of the game. Just about anyone can play. Skill is more important than size. And not counting the goalie, the positions all require similar skills. Players are interchangeable in a way (American) football and baseball players are not. Plus, the relatively simple rules and the short equipment list (ball, shoes) make it easy to play a casual game nearly anywhere with just about any number of players.

Whether it's a pickup match on a humble farm field or a thrilling professional showdown at Chelsea's Stamford Bridge, soccer lovers can't seem to get enough of their beautiful game.

Simple, beautiful, beloved.

TOP SECRET SOCCER

In 1962, Cold War tensions between the United States and the Soviet Union escalated to an alarming level after satellite photographs showed missile launch pads being built in Cuba.

Spy buffs contend that Henry Kissinger, then a consultant for the U.S. Department of State (and a lifelong soccer fan), spotted evidence in the photos that the Soviets were indeed in

Cuba: In addition to the missile sites, he saw soccer fields. The Cubans played baseball. The Soviets played soccer.

FOOTBALL, ANYONE?

Depending on where you are in the world, "football" refers to one of several related but very different games. There's soccer. Then there's the American sport where guys with helmets and pads block, pass, run, and sometimes kick. Then there's rugby, which some aficionados describe as a blend of the two.

The games, though different in many ways, share some similarities as well as a common history. And of course, depending on where you come from, they all share the same name.

AMERICAN FOOTBALL	RUGBY	SOCCER
Super Bowl	World Cup	World Cup
Kickoff	Kickoff, scrum or line-out	Kickoff
Stops and starts	Play on!	Play on!
Offense or defense	Athletes play both O&D	Athletes play both O&D
Popular in the United States	Popular in Europe, Australia, New Zealand, the Caribbean, South Africa	Popular worldwide
Field: 100 x 50 yards	Up to 130 x 100 yards	Typically 75 x 110 yards
(91.4 x 45.7 m)	(118.9 x 91.4 m)	(68.6 x 100.6 m)
Hands	Hands	No hands, except goalie
First played in 1860s	First played in early 1800s	First played in 1697 BC
Touchdowns and field goals	Tries and goals	Goals
Pads and helmets	Limited padding and headgear	Shin guards, plus gloves for goalie
Penalty flags	Cards	Cards
Cheerleaders	Football clubs	Hooligans
Mostly male players	Some women players	Women's teams everywhere

FIFA

Founded in 1904 and based in Zurich, FIFA (the Fédération International de Football Association) is the international governing body of soccer, representing 208 member nations. FIFA administers and markets all worldwide soccer competitions, including the World Cup, and oversees all changes to the rules of the game.

FIFA oversees several regional associations, each with its own championship:

- Union of European Football Associations (UEFA)—UEFA Championship

- Confederation Africaine de Football (CAF)—African Cup of Nations

- Asian Football Confederation (AFC)—Asian Cup

- Confederacion Sudamericana de Futbol (CONMEBOL)—Copa America

- Confederation of North, Central American and Caribbean Association Football (CONCACAF)—CONCACAF Gold Cup

- Oceania Football Confederation (OFC)—OFC Nations Cup

- Panamerican Football Confederation (PFC)—Panamerican Championship

- Union Arab de Football Association (UAFA)—Arab Nations Cup

- Gulf Football Union (GFU)—West Asian Football Federation Championship

THE FIFA WORLD CUP

The World Cup is soccer's Super Bowl. Better yet, since it involves the national teams of thirty-two countries played in the host country over a period of about a month (after years of qualifying matches), the World Cup is the Super Bowl, the World Series, and the Olympics all rolled into one.

Other world championships organized by FIFA include the Under-17 and Under-20 Youth World Championships, the Club World Championships, the Women's World Cup, and the Under-19 Women's World Championship.

THE PROS

Most soccer-playing countries field as many as four professional divisions, the First Division being the top rung. Players move up and down the ladder according to their progress, and some even move sideways when they are transferred (traded) from one club to another.

One of the top leagues in the world is England's Premier League, which features storied clubs such as Manchester United, Arsenal, and Liverpool, among others. Italy's Serie A boasts famous names such as Juventus, Milan, Inter, and Roma. In Argentina's Division I, Boca Juniors or River Plate often take home the title.

Every year, international football fans watch their favorite clubs vie for the most prestigious prizes in their sport, including the European Cup, contested between UEFA Champions League teams; the Liberitadores Cup, the South American version of the European Cup; and the Intercontinental Cup (also known as the "Toyota Cup"), played between the winners of the European and South American club competitions.

NATIONAL TEAMS

Almost every country in the world has a national soccer team, an all-star side comprising the best players from different leagues. Although these days it's not uncommon to see English attackers playing on pro teams in the United States or Brazilian midfielders hitting the pitch for pay in Italy, players may compete for only one national team—the team of their home country.

National teams compete against each other in the Olympics, the World Cup, and other tournaments, as well as occasional exhibition

England's Arsenal is one of many storied clubs.

matches known as "friendlies." Then, in many cases, players return to their regular clubs.

There is a very simple reason why fans get so fanatical about the World Cup and other competitions featuring play between national teams: The games are country vs. country. National pride is on the line.

It's not just a game. It's a matter of pride.

SOREN KNOWS SOCCER

On November 13, 1985, Danish midfielder Soren Lerby became the first soccer player to play for two different teams in two different countries on the same day. First, he contributed mightily to Denmark's World Cup qualifying match against Ireland before departing in the fifty-eighth minute with his club ahead 3–1. (Denmark won 4–1). He then flew to West Germany in his club's private jet to join his team, Bayern Munich, for a third-round cup game. (They tied 1–1). —*Soccer's Most Wanted* by John Snyder

Soccer—A Celebrity Magnet?

Among soccer's many claims to fame are the scores of famous folks who have embraced the game over the years. Luminaries such as Governor Arnold Schwarzenegger, who helped finance a new stadium in his hometown of Graz, Austria; Elton John, an on-again, off-again co-owner of England's Watford Club; and Drew Carey, part-owner of the new Seattle MLS franchise, are all hard-core supporters. Others, such as Spike Lee, who coaches his son's team, are learning to love it.

Some of these famous folks aren't just fans or backers. They are . . . or were . . . players:

- Oliver Cromwell, Sir Walter Scott, and kings of Scotland, England, and France all played soccer.

- Revolutionary icon Che Guevara, the last Shah of Iran, Reza Pahlavi, and former president George Herbert Walker Bush could dribble with the best of them.

- Pope John Paul II was a goalie for the State Secondary School for Boys in Poland.

- Crooner Julio Iglesias, reggae star Bob Marley, funnyman Robin Williams, talk show host Jon Stewart, and actor Matthew Broderick all held their own on the pitch.

- Actors Sean Connery (Scotland) and Anthony LaPaglia (Australia) were pros in their native countries.

- *Melrose Place* star Andrew Shue played for the L.A. Galaxy.

Many stars of other sports—such as NBA standout Steve Nash (British Columbia National High School Soccer Player of the Year), MLB star Nomar Garciaparra (who's also Mia Hamm's husband), and NFL punter Sean Landeta—once considered making soccer their number one game. One way or another, soccer is the common denominator among every one of these A-list names:

Prince Albert of Monaco
Ed Asner
Antonio Banderas
Boris Becker
George Clooney
Kevin Costner
Rodney Dangerfield
Def Leppard bandmates
Johnny Depp
Cameron Diaz
P. Diddy

Placido Domingo
Dr. Dre
Peter Frampton
Michael Jackson
Samuel L. Jackson
Mick Jagger
Magic Johnson
Elton John
Henry Kissinger
Spike Lee
Mike Myers
Michael Moore

Oasis bandmates Liam and Noel Gallagher
Queen Elizabeth II
Stephen Rea
Arnold Schwarzenegger
Paul Simon
Sylvester Stallone
Rod Stewart
Mike Tyson
Weezer bandmates
Franco Zeffirelli

Some twenty million Americans of all ages and genders play soccer. Some four million play soccer on a weekly basis.

SOCCER STATESIDE

Perhaps because the team was made up mostly of Scottish and English immigrants—soccer players from way back—the U. S. national team started out strong during the early part of the twentieth century. At the inaugural World Cup in 1930, the Americans won their first two matches, besting both Belgium and Paraguay 3–0. But it would be twenty years before they notched another win when they beat a heavily favored English team in the "miracle match" of 1950.

Several dismal decades followed. Then, in 1990, the United States qualified for the World Cup final round for the first time since 1950 when they beat Trinidad and Tobago 1–0. The match was a thriller—both teams remained scoreless until Paul Caliguri booted in a goal from 30 yards (27.4 m) in the thirty-first minute. Unfortunately, the United States lost its next three matches and was eliminated from the competition. But no doubt about it, a spark had been ignited.

The 1990s were a defining decade for American soccer. In 1991, the U.S. Men won the Gold Cup (defeating Honduras 4–3) to determine the North and Central American/Caribbean championship. Also in 1991, the United States won the very first Women's World Cup (defeating Norway 2–1 in the championship match) and dug in deep as an international soccer powerhouse.

The U.S. Men won their first World Cup final round match in forty-four years when they defeated Colombia 2–1 in 1994. (The Americans lost 1–0 to Brazil in the second round.) In 1995, they defeated Chile at the Copa America in Uruguay for their first win in South American since 1950. The squad followed with a 3–0 upset over Argentina and a quarterfinal win over Mexico before losing to Brazil in the semifinals.

The 1998 World Cup was disappointing for U.S. soccer fans as the national team failed to win a single match. But there was some redemption that same year when D.C. United became the first American team to win the CONCACAF Gold Cup. (They beat Mexico 1–0.) Later that same year, D.C. United did it again when they became the first U.S. club to win the Interamerican Cup, 2–0, over Brazil's Vasco da Gama.

AMERICAN PROFESSIONALS

In 1996, Major League Soccer (MLS), the top-tier pro league in North America, began play with ten teams in the United States and Canada. As of 2010, there will be sixteen teams playing in three divisions, Eastern, Central, and Western:

Houston Dynamo	New England Revolution	Chivas USA
Chicago Fire	D.C. United	FC Dallas
New York Red Bulls	Kansas City Wizards	Columbus Crew
Colorado Rapids	Los Angeles Galaxy	Real Salt Lake
Toronto FC	San Jose Earthquakes	Seattle Sounders
Philadelphia (2010)		

Though the league contracted in 2001, eliminating franchises in Miami and Tampa Bay, it has resumed expansion with plans to add two more teams by 2012. Contenders include St. Louis, Atlanta, Montreal, Detroit, Portland, San Diego, Vancouver, another try at a Miami franchise, and an additional team in the New York area.

MLS teams play a thirty-game regular season schedule that kicks off in March and finishes with the championship match, the MLS Cup, in November. Teams put together their rosters mostly by way of the Superdraft, a process where players are selected in a combination of college and supplemental drafts. Other players may be discovered and signed at other times during the year by coaches and scouts. And, since the Designated Player Rule went into effect in 2006, teams may sign up to two players (usually international stars) above the salary cap. This rule enabled the L.A. Galaxy to acquire English star David Beckham in 2007, resulting in an enormous burst of publicity for the league.

Among the most promising signs for MLS and its future growth is the youth development initiative introduced in 2006. Each team is now required to sponsor a development squad of youth players with the ultimate goal of signing two "homegrown" players from that group every year.

Add that to the list of the league's other accomplishments—the hiring of full-time, professional referees and the construction of more soccer-specific stadiums—and soccer fans don't dare say it out loud, but . . . could pro soccer be in the U.S.A. to stay?

A DIFFERENT KIND OF CAP

As of 2008, the minimum salary for an MLS player was $33,000 per year. (Developmental players make a minimum of $12,900 per year.) Although it's not unusual to see a player making $100,000 or even $150,000 per year, the average player makes much less. Also, the disparity between paychecks is huge considering that David Beckham—who was paid $6.5 million by the L.A. Galaxy in 2008—has a dozen teammates making $33,000.

Note: Beckham is the best-paid "footballer" in the world. According to *Forbes* magazine, between team salaries (Galaxy and Real Madrid) and endorsements, his earnings in 2007 were $49 million. The second highest earner worldwide was Manchester United's Cristiano Ronaldo, with $19 million from salary and endorsements. Number 3? A.C. Milan's Kaka at $18 million.

THE FITS AND STARTS OF PRO SOCCER

Before the MLS got going, there were a dozen previous attempts to kick off professional soccer in the United States in the last century. The most successful recent effort came courtesy of the North American Soccer League (NASL), which was the result of a merger between two leagues, the United Soccer Association (USA) and the National Professional Soccer League (NPSL), and lasted from 1967 to 1985. Prior to that, the American Soccer League (ASL) tried three times (1921–1933, 1934–1983, and 1988–89) to establish a lasting pro league.

Other leagues that have either merged with others or simply ceased operations include: the United Soccer League (USL), the NPSL (second incarnation), the Major Indoor Soccer League (since restarted), the Western Soccer League (WSL), the Lone Star Soccer Alliance (LSSA), the Continental Indoor Soccer League (CISL), the Eastern Indoor Soccer League (EISL), the World Indoor Soccer League (WISL), and the soon-to-be restarted Women's United Soccer Association (WUSA).

HERE COME THE GIRLS

According to Pia Sundhage, Swedish soccer star turned U.S. Women's National Team coach, women weren't always welcome on the field: "When I started playing, I played with boys, and I wasn't supposed to play because I was a girl."

The same was true for many of her female contemporaries around the world. As recently as the early 1970s, there were virtually no opportunities for girls under the age of 18 to play

You go, girl!

The U.S. National Women's Team inspired soccer-playing girls worldwide.

soccer. Outside of intramural sports, college women didn't fare much better. But as the decade went on, women's soccer began to gather steam on several continents.

In the United States, part of the reason for the increase in opportunities to play soccer may be directly traced to 1972 and the passage of Title IX, the education amendment declaring that no person shall be excluded from participation in any activity receiving federal financial assistance. This amendment, which forces schools to offer parity between men's and women's programs, made (and continues to make) an enormous impact on women's sports at both the high-school and the college level.

Many of the first U.S. Women's National Team players, who played their first game in 1985, were products of Title IX. The team went on to win gold in 1996 at the first women's Olympic soccer match in Atlanta. Next, they made history by winning the first-ever Women's World Cup in 1991. A few years later, the U.S. Women—already on the world's radar—officially put soccer on the American map when they bested China to win the World Cup at the Rose Bowl in Pasadena, California, in 1999. More than ninety thousand spectators watched in person (and some forty million tuned in on TV) as Brandi Chastain knocked in the winning penalty kick and whipped off her shirt in a joyous celebration.

Today, the U.S. Women are consistently among the best players in the world, with a long list of big wins: two Women's World Cups (1991 and 1999), two Olympic Women's Tournaments (1996 and 2004), and six Algarve Cups (2000, 2003, 2004, 2005, 2007, and 2008). The United States Under-19 (U-19) Women's National Team also won the inaugural FIFA U-19 Women's World Championship in 2002.

Stats, accolades, and championships are wonderful. But perhaps the most exciting thing about the success of the women's team is the inspiration it provides to young girls across the United States and the world.

Today, who doesn't know a girl who plays soccer? There are co-ed and all-girls recreational teams in almost every city. Almost every high

Women's soccer is everywhere today.

school fields a girls' soccer team. And if a player is really ambitious, she can try out for the Olympic Development Program or set her sights on playing at a college powerhouse, such as the University of North Carolina, UCLA, or Notre Dame. Soccer is the most popular collegiate sport for women; the National Collegiate Athletic Association (NCAA) lists more than 20,000 women soccer players on its rosters. (The number of men is just slightly lower.)

These days, if a girl wants to play, she can play.

She can even go pro.

Despite the efforts of the 1920s-era Dick-Kerr Ladies Professional Team, made up of female British munitions factory workers, it took sixty years to launch the women's pro game. The world's first professional league for women, the Women's United Soccer Association (WUSA), began play in 2001 with eight teams and many of the sport's biggest stars, including Michelle Akers, Julie Foudy, Mia Hamm, Kristine Lilly, and Briana Scurry. American players made up the majority of the rosters, although up to four international players were allowed on each of the teams: Atlanta Beat, Boston Breakers, Carolina Courage, New York Power, Philadelphia Charge, San Diego Spirit, San Jose CyberRays, and Washington Freedom.

The WUSA completed three full seasons, but in 2003, due to disappointing earnings, they ceased operations. Still, fans of women's soccer have reason to be hopeful. The league (newly named Women's Professional Soccer) plans to resume play in 2009.

Mia Hamm, the most recognizable women's soccer player in the world, has scored more goals than any player—man or woman—in the history of the sport.

FEARLESS FANS

After the Islamic Revolution in 1979, females were forbidden to watch soccer in Iran's 120,000-seat Azadi stadium. (The name translates as "freedom.") It 's reported, though, that many women sneaked in dressed as men.

In 1987, Ayatollah Ruhollah Khomeini declared that women could watch soccer on TV, but that wasn't enough. In 1997, when the Iranian national team qualified for the World Cup for the first time in almost twenty years, thousands of

women stormed the Azadi and overwhelmed the police, who eventually let them in to celebrate. Today, Iranian women not only watch but play; they even sent a club to the Women's Soccer Championship in Jordan in 2008.

After the 1993 World Cup playoffs, Saudi Arabia, which spent more on team preparation than any other country, awarded its players with massive cash bonuses and gifts of cars and land.

U.S. SOCCER

The United States Soccer Federation, also known as U.S. Soccer, has been the governing body of American soccer since 1913. Originally named the U.S. Football Association, then, until 1973, the U.S. Soccer Football Association, the Chicago-based organization oversees all things soccer in the United States, from the recreational to the competitive level. U.S. Soccer should be the first stop for any player. Coaches and referees will also find it helpful to check out the numerous resources, including licensing and education programs that take place year-round.

The many affiliates of U.S. Soccer include U.S. Youth Soccer, the American Youth Soccer Organization (AYSO), Soccer Association for Youth (SAY), US Club Soccer, and the United States Adult Soccer

Association (USASA). A major focus for the organization is the U.S. Soccer Foundation, which provides grants, financial support, and loans to help develop coaches, players, and referees, especially in economically disadvantaged urban areas.

U.S. Soccer counts the 2003 unveiling of the National Training Center at the Home Depot Center in Carson, California, and the 2007 debut of the U.S. Soccer Development Academy as two of its major recent accomplishments. The Development Academy is a boys' program consisting of seventy-five of the top youth soccer clubs in the United States. Each academy club is selected by the U.S. National Team and fields two teams, one for players under 16, one for players under 18. Academy clubs are divided into eight conferences of eight teams, which play thirty matches during the eight-month season. The winner of each conference plays in the Academy Finals at the Home Depot Center.

A higher level of play now means a higher level of play later.

According to John Hackworth, U.S. Under-17 Men's National Team head coach, the ultimate goal of the academy is to develop elite players. "We want players to move towards an environment where they are practicing three to five times a week, compared to once or twice, and playing high-level meaningful and competitive matches every week," he says. "This setting will allow them to learn and develop at a much higher rate."

Start 'Em Young

According to U.S. Youth Soccer, since 1990, registration among its teams has climbed nearly 90 percent, totaling 3.2 million players. It seems that just about every kid wants to play soccer. So, on the off chance a child isn't already on a team, where does a player or a soccer mom or dad begin?

Start 'em young.

Many kids start playing at a very young age. U.S. Women's National Team goalkeeper Briana Scurry began playing at age 9. Mia Hamm started kicking the ball around with her brother just after she learned to walk. It's not unusual to see young players suiting up for organized play as early as age 4. Most coaches say this is not too young as long as the environment is relaxed and the kids are having fun. Often, out of convenience or necessity (not enough players on game day), girls and boys play together. Again, coaches say this is fine up until age 12 or 13, when kids' bodies begin to change.

U.S. Youth Soccer is the largest governing body for youth soccer in the United States, but other governing bodies also count dozens

Why Soccer?

"You get to kick it really hard!"—*Ben Sanchez, age 5, Hollywood, Florida, who plays with his brothers Sebi and Nico.*

In the early years, boys and girls often play together.

WHY SOCCER?

"It's a fun, running sport. I love it when my team—Flamengo—makes a goal. Flamengo is one of the four big Rio teams. Since I'm their fan, that makes me a Flamenguista!"—*Eleanor King, age 9, Rio de Janeiro, Brazil*

of leagues and thousands of players on their rosters. Parents simply need to do some research to find out what groups are available in their area, keeping in mind the philosophies and goals of the different organizations. (For example, the AYSO is guided by the motto that "Everyone Plays." Some teams, especially those that are part of competitive travel clubs, will have a very different approach.)

US Youth Soccer is organized into four national regions, fifty-five state associations (large states such as California have more than one), and hundreds of leagues. Leagues comprise a certain number of clubs that often list more than one team (for different ages and levels of play) under their banner. Club teams play each other locally if they are recreational ("rec") teams or in state or regional tournaments if they are travel soccer teams.

Moving On Up

As soccer moms know all too well, travel soccer is a huge commitment. So beware: Talented players may be asked to join premier teams, composed of the best players from various leagues in a certain age group. This means the player may be participating on his home team *and* a premier team, often traveling for both.

As a player moves up the youth soccer ladder, he may try out or be picked for a league select team, an Olympic Development team, a regional team, or ultimately a national team. It all depends on his commitment to the game—and, often, his parents' sense of direction.

Talented players take it on the road.

Championships

Every summer, the top club teams in the United States compete for the top prize during the U.S. Youth Soccer National Championship Series. Both boys and girls first compete in six age groups (Under-14, Under-15, Under-16, Under-17, Under-18, and Under-19) during a series of regional tournaments. Then the regional winners compete in the nationals, which are staged in a different city every year.

Commitment.

Why Soccer?

"Ever since I could walk I just fell in love with that little round ball. I live, breathe, and play soccer. It's the most amazing sport in the world to me. Not only does it take dedication and heart; it's one of the toughest sports out there. You have to be in such incredible shape to play and last in a game. Many people don't realize how much running there really is. Every time I step onto the field, a rush of adrenalin bursts through my body. The feeling is amazing, and I never want to lose it."—*Kayde Hensley, age 18, Fallbrook, California*

There are dozens of other prestigious tournaments for youth players held every year, including the U.S.A. Cup (in Minnesota) and the Potomac Cup (in Washington, D.C.) Often, college coaches and scouts attend the tournaments to search for future recruits.

High School

It used to be that most high schools only fielded a soccer team in the spring, if they fielded one at all. (No one wanted soccer to attempt to compete with football.) These days, there is plenty of room for both sports, and soccer is often played in both spring and fall. When teams are sanctioned by a school, they come under the umbrella of the National Federation of State High School Associations (NFHS). Although high-school seasons tend to be shorter than club seasons, most of the rules are the same.

CAMPS

If soccer players just haven't gotten enough of soccer on their high school, club, and travel teams, or if they want to improve their game or fine-tune a specific skill, attending a soccer camp (usually in the summer or during other school breaks) is a fantastic idea. There are dozens of quality camps to choose from. Players or parents can ask their coaches or search online for camps that fit their needs. It's important to ask specific questions regarding the age and skill level of other players, the qualifications of the coaches, and the focus of the camp.

Players may want to attend specialized camps, such as those exclusively for goalies.

SOCCER VENUES

Many of the largest sports stadiums in the world are soccer stadiums. Throughout the twentieth century, the size of soccer stadiums seemed to grow in direct proportion to the popularity of the game: Both kept getting bigger and bigger. In order to accommodate the largest number of fans, many in search of cheap tickets, numerous venues in the 1960s, 1970s, and 1980s began to designate large standing-room-only sections or add temporary bleachers for big matches. Further, many of

All eyes on the pitch.

According to FC Dallas' (MLS) Brek Shea's mom, he was born to play soccer. "His first word was ball," she said. "His very first word. Before 'mom.'"

the older stadiums failed to upgrade their facilities for safety purposes. This turned out to be a dangerous trend, as witnessed by the collapse of the stands at Ibrox Stadium in Glasgow, Scotland, in 1971 and the tragic flash fire at Valley Parade in Bradford, England, in 1985. With the goal of increasing crowd control and safety, some stadiums have actually been downsized; the trend for new structures is to design smaller venues with seats rather than community seating benches while eliminating other elements such as standing-room-only terraces and temporary bleachers.

The mighty London-based team Arsenal had some truly lowly beginnings. According to Soccer's Most Wanted, the team's first game was played on a field that had an open sewer running through it. They soon moved up to playing on a pig farm on the edge of a marsh. Until recently, they played at Highbury Stadium, a storied place that survived German bombs in WWII and decades of rowdy fans. Highbury was recently converted into a luxury apartment building, and today Arsenal plays at its new facility, Emirates Stadium.

Here are some of the world's biggest and brightest soccer venues:

MARACANA STADIUM: Rio de Janeiro, Brazil, 165,000 (former capacity: 220,000)

RUNGNADO: Pyongyang, North Korea, 150,000

SALT LAKE: New Delhi, India, 120,000

NOU CAMP: Barcelona, Spain, 109,815

SANTIAGO BERNABEU: Madrid, Spain, 87,000

OLYMPIC STADIUM: Munich, Germany, 63,000

AZTECA: Mexico City, Mexico, 106,000

HAMPDEN PARK: Glasgow, Scotland, 52,208 (Hampden Park formerly held nearly 150,000 fans and was the largest stadium in the world until Maracana was built in 1950.)

LUZHNIKI STADIUM: Moscow, Russia, 80,840

CENTENARIO: Montevideo, Uruguay, 73,609

STUDIO GIUSSEPPE MEAZZA: Milan, Italy, 84,847

ROSE BOWL: Pasadena, California, 100,000 (The Rose Bowl was originally built in 1922 for college football's New Year's Day Rose Bowl. It is the only stadium in the world to host both a men's and a women's World Cup final.)

WEMBLEY: London, England, 90,000 (Built in 1923, the recently refurbished and rebuilt Wembley formerly held 126,000.)

An Arsenal fan's colors.

INSIDE GAME

Partly out of necessity (snow-covered fields in winter) and partly out of preference (some players favor this version of the game), soccer is often played indoors. The official FIFA-sanctioned name for indoor soccer is "futsal" and the rules are slightly different. The game may be played on artificial turf or on hardwood courts, depending on the facility. In Mexico, indoor soccer (known there as "futbol rapido") is so popular, mostly due to the fast-moving nature of the game, that indoor soccer fields are actually built outdoors.

Many pro, semi-pro, and amateur indoor soccer leagues have formed, folded, and re-formed over the years. The Major Indoor Soccer League (MISL) has been the top professional indoor soccer league in the United States since 2001. Nine teams play a season that runs from October to April. The Premier Arena Soccer League serves as the minor-league version of MISL. Other indoor leagues include the American Indoor Soccer League, the Canadian Major Indoor Soccer League, and Campeonato Nacional de Liga de Futbol Indoor.

SOCCER ON TV

Not that long ago, soccer fans in the United States were hard-pressed to find soccer on TV. Hard core followers sought out World Cup satellite broadcasts at their favorite English pub, often in the middle of the night. Then with the explosion of cable and satellite TV and the rising popularity of the game in this country, things began to change. Some forty million people watched the 1999 Women's World Cup final between the United States and China, making it the most-watched soccer game in American TV history. Picking up some of that momentum, the WUSA was broadcast on TNT, CNNSI, ESPN2, PAXTV, and various local and regional sports channels from 2001 through 2003. Today, there are networks devoted only to soccer, including the Fox Soccer Channel, which broadcasts MLS matches, news, and other soccer programming 24/7. ESPN, ESPN2, and various networks also regularly broadcast MLS games.

Several Internet sites list daily TV listings (http://www.ussoccer. com, http://www.livesoccertv.com, http://msn.foxsports.com) or pubs around the world that feature games on TV (http://www.soccerbars. com) so fans can find everything from college and youth games to Barclay's Premier League playoff matches, just about any day of the week.

GAME ON

Can't make it to the game? Another cool place to watch (besides the stadium) is in a soccer-friendly pub. Here are just a few, along with their claims to fame:

- **The Grapes Bar.** (Glasgow, Scotland) Headquarters for Rangers FC fans. Cheer for other clubs (or wear their colors) at your peril.

- **The Shed.** (London, England) Longtime favorite of Chelsea Football Club fans.

- **Ginger's Ale House.** (Chicago, Illinois) Four-time winner of U.S. Soccer's "Best Soccer Pub" award.

- **Three Lions Pub.** (Charleston, South Carolina) The best of both worlds—a pub inside Blackbaud Stadium.

- **George & Dragon Pub.** (Seattle, Washington) Hangout for fans of the new Seattle Sounders franchise, including co-owner Drew Carey.

Pele scored his thousandth goal on November 19, 1969, at Maracana Stadium in Rio. (A plaque at the stadium commemorates the achievement and calls it "The most beautiful game ever.")

"I'm a fan. I can see the beauty of the game. Hopefully it will grow here in the States. I follow it as much as I can. I got the satellite."—ACTOR, DIRECTOR, AND YOUTH SOCCER COACH SPIKE LEE

From the pitch to the tube.

WHY SOCCER?

"You can show boys that you know a sport and can be good playing it. I also like the feeling of being out there and trying your best in what you love."—Isabelle King, age

In the mid 1990s, soccer fans in Brazil used to bring animals such as dogs, turtles, and other pets, many of them decked out in team gear, to Flamengo games in honor of star player Edmundo, who was nicknamed "The Animal." Then the government declared the practice illegal.

"Potentially in the States, soccer can be as big as it is everywhere else in the world."—DAVID BECKHAM

2: THE STORY OF SOCCER

Who Kicked It First . . . and Where and When

No one claims to know the exact moment in history when someone (a caveman? an ancient warrior?) kicked a ball around for the very first time. Just for fun. There are no documents to mark the day when that same guy kicked the "ball" (which could have been a coconut, a round piece of wood, or an enemy's severed head) through a goal—or the day he rounded up some friends and started keeping score.

Historians do agree, though, that many people in many different parts of the world played a game that looked something like soccer hundreds— or even thousands—of years ago.

COCONUTS, PIG BLADDERS, AND SKULLS

Military manuals from the Tsin (255–206 BC) and Han (206 BC–AD 220) dynasties describe Chinese soldiers playing a kicking game called *tsu chu*. This game, which was really more of a military skill drill than a form of amusement, featured players kicking or using their chests, backs, heads, and shoulders (but no hands) to put a feather-and-hair-stuffed leather ball into a net held taut by bamboo poles. Some historians date this form of the sport even farther back—as early as 1697 BC, when athletes played a similar game to entertain Chinese emperor Huangdi.

Ancient drawings found in Egypt and the Near East depict people running and kicking balls during religious and fertility ceremonies. There is evidence of Eskimos in Alaska and Canada kicking and dribbling a ball stuffed with grass, caribou hair, and moss over the ice through goals spaced out many miles apart.

In Mexico and Central America, people played with balls fashioned from rubber on 50-foot (15.2-m) courts enclosed by high walls. Early inhabitants of several Pacific Islands are known to have played games that involved kicking "balls" such as coconuts, oranges, and pig bladders. There is evidence that the Vikings played too. And when European explorers first landed in the New World, they discovered Native Americans playing a soccer-like game on the beaches.

In England, the country that would eventually define the sport, it is said that an entire village joined in to defeat a visiting Roman team at soccer and run them out of town in AD 217. An even more popular—and grisly—legend says that early English footballers once used a conquered invader's skull as a ball.

SOCCER—WAY BACK WHEN

- *Tsu Chu*—China (255–206 BC). Possibly the first soccer ever documented, more a military skill drill than a game. Players kicked or used their feet, chests, backs, or shoulders to put a feather-and-hair-stuffed leather ball into a net held taut by bamboo poles.

- *Kemari*—Japan (AD second–third century). Also called "kenatt." A circular football game, more ceremonial than competitive. Players passed the ball to each other in a very small space, trying to keep the ball from touching the ground.

- *Episkyros*—An early Greek game, a lively forerunner to modern soccer. Trickery won more games than skillful footwork.

- *Harpastum*—An early Roman game played with a small ball on a rectangular field. Here, too, trickery was a key component.

- *Tlatchi*—An early Central and South American soccer precursor.

- *Aqsaqtuk*—An early Eskimo game played in what is now Canada and Alaska. Teams from different villages played against each other on ice. As the legend goes, goals were sometimes as much as ten miles apart.

- *Shrovetide Football*—England (AD third century–present). A rough-and-tumble form of mob football with an unspecified (or unlimited) number of players and often nonexistent rules, still played today—in a less violent manner—on Shrove Tuesday in a number of English towns. Note: A similar game was played in France during the same era.

- *Calcio*—Italy (Renaissance). Athletes dressed in colored livery played this highly choreographed kicking game in Florence and Venice during holidays or at important events.

Blowing up the football for calcio in Renaissance Italy.

- *Pasuckuakohowog*—North America (sixteenth century). European explorers found natives playing this game (translation: "they gather to play ball with the foot") on enormous fields stretching half a mile wide and one mile from goal to goal. Games sometimes involved up to one thousand players, lasted for days, and culminated with a great feast.

MOTHER ENGLAND

Running rough and rowdy in the streets of London, circa 1312.

Games that look like soccer's ancestors can be traced to many parts of the ancient world, but there is no question that the modern game took shape in Great Britain.

A rough-and-tumble form of mob football (or soccer) was being played in different parts of England as early as the third century AD. Emphasis on "mob": the number of players was basically unlimited, and rules were mostly nonexistent. (A much less violent version of this game, known as "Shrovetide Football," is still played on Shrove Tuesday in a number of English towns.)

For several centuries, games looked more like riots than sporting events. Players were sometimes maimed or even killed in the course of play, and teams often spent as much time looting and vandalizing the town where they played as they did advancing the ball. For this reason, soccer was outlawed numerous times over the years. It's no surprise that the game did not evolve much during this era. Who was going to sit down and write up rules for a game that was illegal in the first place?

Lucien Laurent of France scored the very first goal in the first-ever World Cup in 1930.

Soccer Outlaws

During soccer's formative years, the game was not always viewed by the powers that be as a wholesome pursuit. In centuries past, European kings, queens, and local lords often denounced the game—and sometimes declared it illegal.

- In 1314, the Lord Mayor of London issued a proclamation forbidding football within the city. In 1331, King Edward passed even harsher measures to suppress this "public nuisance."

- During the Hundred Years War (between England and France from 1338–1453) Kings Edward III, Richard II, Henry IV, and Henry V all declared football illegal. Their reason? Playing the game kept their subjects from practicing more useful military disciplines, such as archery.

- England's Queen Elizabeth passed a law whereby soccer players were to be "jailed for a week and obliged to do penance in church."

- In Scotland in 1424, King James I proclaimed in Parliament "that na man play at the fute-ball" (no man shall play football).

- In sixteenth-century England, the rise of puritanism led to a backlash against soccer and all frivolous pursuits, especially if they violated the Sabbath. Soccer was legally prohibited on Sundays, a ban that remained in effect for three hundred years.

- In the 1920s, Iranian mullahs ordered that soccer players in the villages be pelted with stones.

But despite the best effort of the monarchs, football remained a passion of the people.

Ruling the Mob

From the 1300s to the 1800s, the violence lessened somewhat, but soccer remained a mob game, meaning that teams didn't consist of a set number of players, but rather played with whatever cluster of people happened to be on hand. Rules were still loose, when they were followed at all.

During the 1800s, participation in soccer increased as the United Kingdom and surrounding countries became more industrialized. Working-class people had more leisure time and were looking for

Fifteen teams competed in the first Challenge Cup in 1871. The Wanderers won the trophy, valued at twenty pounds.

games to play. Improved railway systems meant players could travel to matches. Even rising literacy contributed as newspapers gave more coverage to organized sports, especially soccer.

On the other side of the tracks, society's elite also began to embrace the game, especially during the early to mid 1800s, when advocates at Britain's prestigious public schools put forth the idea that sports were good for students' minds and bodies and thus a positive addition to the curriculum. Regarding soccer in particular, some proponents argued that at least the sport constituted a useful distraction from less desirable occupations, such as heavy drinking and gambling. Soon, participation in soccer was compulsory in many schools.

Clearly, mob rules were no longer enough; the sport needed some structure. At first, each school made its own rules depending on the particular playing space it had available. For example, schools such as Charterhouse, Westminster, and Eton played on smaller playgrounds, some that happened to be paved and surrounded by brick walls. Obviously, this limited the number of players who could occupy the field and the type of contact they could make with one another, so it makes sense that players mostly kicked the ball, as opposed to running with it and tackling each other. Schools such as Cheltenham and Rugby, on the other hand, played on expansive outdoor fields, so players had room to pick up the ball and run with it. Since there were no paved surfaces or brick walls for players to slam into, it's not surprising that a rougher version of the sport (which eventually became rugby) was developed there.

But in the 1840s, all forms of the game were still considered "football." There were several attempts to standardize the rules, some of which were laughably lax by today's standards: For example, kicking an opponent below the knees was permitted so long as the aggressor or his teammate did not hold the player down while doing so. Then, in 1848, students from several schools met in Cambridge with the goal of further standardizing the rules of the game. Although they agreed on a set of guidelines known as "The Cambridge Rules," it took another fifteen years for things to become official.

On October 26, 1863, eleven English teams sent representatives to the Freemason's Tavern in London to set down rules that would form the basis of the Football Association (FA). During the meeting, the

The Freemason's Tavern is long gone. But the Freemasons Arms is up and running on the original London site.

majority of team leaders spoke in favor of outlawing unruly practices such as shin-kicking, pushing, tripping, and so on. They also expressed a desire to forbid ball carrying and handling of any sort. (This provision took a few years to pass; when it did, the teams from Rugby and several other schools broke off to pursue their own version of the game.)

By the early 1870s, soccer was being played throughout Great Britain. In 1871, the Football Association boasted fifty member teams and held the first major soccer competition, the FA Cup, also known as the "Challenge Cup," to determine a champion. Soon the English FA was joined by associations from Wales, Scotland, and Ireland, and in 1882 the four groups formed the International Football Association Board (IFAB) to regulate their own play and to oversee the inevitable growth of the sport.

The first major issue confronting soccer's new football associations, especially those in the United Kingdom, was professionalism. In the early days of the sport, there was a strict code of amateur play. But as early as the 1870s, some clubs (notably in Lancashire, England) were accused of illicit payments to players. Soon players, especially those from working-class towns, were clamoring to be paid for "broken time" (wages lost when they missed work to play in games). Despite the protests of players in upper-class leagues (for whom pay was not a crucial issue), the English FA sanctioned professionalism in 1884. (Note: Professionalism was slower to evolve around the world. For example, pay for play was not sanctioned in France, Argentina, or Brazil until the 1930s.)

The most goals in World Cup history (fourteen) were scored by West Germany's Gerd Miller: ten in 1970 and four in 1974.

KICKING COUSINS

Besides rugby, soccer claims a couple of other close "football" relatives, namely Australian Rules football (codified in 1885) and Gaelic football (codified in 1865).

- **Aussie Rules football.** This game, played mainly in Australia, closely resembles rugby, with its kicking, running, tackling, and oval-shaped ball. However, teams are made up of eighteen players per side, and there are other differences; for example, Aussie football includes a play called a "mark," where a player who catches a ball from a kick is automatically awarded a free kick, and it has no offside rule.

- **Gaelic football.** This game, played mainly in Ireland, also closely resembles rugby. Players (fifteen per side) attempt to send the round, soccer-like ball through the goal by kicking or striking it with their hands.

SOCCER FOR EXPORT

In the late 1800s, British sailors and traders helped kick off a truly global expansion, introducing football to ports around the world. Soon, football—or soccer—was a near-worldwide phenomenon (with a few holdouts, including the United States). Between 1890 and 1910, dozens of nations from France and Hungary to Brazil and Uruguay formed their own teams, competitions, and associations. Then, in 1904, France and six other European nations formed the Fédération Internationale de Football Association (FIFA), which remains the international governing body of the sport to this day.

THE "GAME OF IMMIGRANTS"

The first organized soccer team in the United States, the Oneida Football Club of Boston, was launched in 1862. But soccer failed to take off in the United States in the late nineteenth and early twentieth centuries the way it did around the world. Why? Historians offer several theories.

1950s matches played at the Metropolitan Oval soccer complex (a.k.a. the "Met Oval") in Maspeth, Queens, New York City. *Courtesy of the National Soccer Hall of Fame.*

According to Bill Murray, author of *The World's Game: The History of Soccer,* "Soccer remained a backwater in the U.S., the game of recent immigrants, and as such one that was frowned upon by parents who wanted their sons to become good Americans." Instead, aspiring athletes embraced American-born games such as football, basketball, and baseball.

Other theories point to difficulties encountered by potential pro leagues. For example, one early league failed because the teams were effectively slapped together by baseball team owners looking to fill their stadiums during the off-season. Still another explanation is that soccer lacked a history in America. There were no passionate fans attached to and bound to support local teams, as there were in Europe.

However, there were a few notable exceptions. New England's industrial region, especially around Fall River, Massachusetts, was home to dozens of teams in the late 1800s

Stan Chesney, star of the New York Americans, and the Brookhattan (New York City) team at play in the 1940s. Great action but not yet a major American pastime. *Courtesy of the National Soccer Hall of Fame.*

and even gave birth to the first soccer governing organization in the United States, the American Football Association. In St. Louis, a soccer hotbed then and now, the Kensingtons (founded in 1890) fielded the first all-American-born team and repeatedly contributed players to U.S. national teams over the years. Soccer leagues popped up out west (mainly in California), and by 1912, there were organized collegiate leagues in twelve states.

Still, despite a brief surge in popularity after the United States was accepted into FIFA in 1913, soccer failed to catch on in this country. Decades would pass before that would change for good.

The first organized American soccer team, the Oneida Football Club of Boston, (founded in 1862 by Gerrit Smith Miller), was made up of Boston-area high-school players who played three undefeated seasons and didn't allow a single goal. Their games were played on Boston Common, where in 1925 the seven surviving members placed a monument to commemorate the club, which disbanded in 1865.

—*SOCCER'S MOST WANTED* BY JOHN SNYDER

THE OLYMPICS

The first modern Olympic Games in Athens in 1896 featured "football" as a demonstration sport, but the first official men's tournament was not played until the 1908 London Games, where England beat Denmark 2–0 to win the gold. Soccer has been a key event at nearly every Olympics since.

When Uruguay took the gold medal in both 1924 and 1928, South America announced itself to the world as an emerging soccer continent. Uruguay's success was part of the reason it was selected to host the first World Cup two years later.

Other milestones include the introduction of the women's tournament at Atlanta in 1996, with the U.S. team taking the top prize, and the upset at the men's tournament that same year, when Nigeria beat Brazil in the semifinal and then defeated the favored Argentine team in the final (3–2) to become the first African team to win gold.

The Olympic soccer tournament remains an enormously popular event among fans. At the Moscow Games in 1980, nearly two million spectators watched the soccer matches. Four years later, one and a half million fans watched the games in Los Angeles, setting the stage for the United States to host the World Cup in 1994.

The U.S. team has competed in the men's finals twelve times, including five straight tournaments from 1984 to 2000. After the U.S.

Women took the first-ever gold medal in Atlanta in 1996, they won silver in 2000, then reclaimed the gold in 2004.

Throughout its history, the biggest challenge facing Olympic soccer—like other sports—has been determining what constitutes an amateur. (In the 1932 games, because officials could not agree on the definition of the term, no soccer tournament was held at all.) The fact that some countries, specifically in the former Soviet Bloc from the early 1960s until the late 1980s, subsidized the training of their players remained a constant subject of debate. Another sore subject was the corporate endorsements and sponsorships of some players from Western countries that arguably constituted "pay."

As of the 1984 games, professionals have been permitted to compete in the Olympics, with some restrictions. Another change: Prior to 2008, the number of players over the age of 23 permitted to play was restricted. Those restrictions have been lifted, allowing countries to choose from a pool of their very best players.

The U.S. team enters Centennial Stadium for the 1930 World Cup. *Courtesy of the National Soccer Hall of Fame.*

THE GLOBAL GRANDDADDY OF THEM ALL

The FIFA World Cup, or, as millions and millions of fans know it, simply the "World Cup," began in 1930 as a tournament between national teams. (Host team Uruguay won the final 4–2 against Argentina that year.) The event has been played every four years since, except when it was interrupted by World War II in 1942 and the repercussions of the war in 1946.

What is now the most prestigious international soccer championship and the most popular sports event in the world actually got off to a rocky start. In 1930, it was an enormous undertaking to host such an event; Uruguay was ultimately given the nod because organizers in that country were willing to accept the financial risk. At the time, commercial air travel was still a new phenomenon, so European teams willing to make the long journey to South America had to commit to a three-week boat trip, not to mention enormous travel expenses.

For this reason, only four European teams traveled to Uruguay: France, Belgium, Yugoslavia, and Romania. This meant that many of the top soccer nations, including England, Scotland, Italy, and Hungary, were not represented.

1930 U.S. World Cup stars Adelino "Billy" Gonsalves (a.k.a. the Babe Ruth of American soccer) and Bertrand Patenaude (the first player to register a "hat trick" in World Cup play). *Courtesy of the National Soccer Hall of Fame.*

Much like the Olympics, the World Cup has not been immune to boycotts. England did not compete in 1934 or 1938 because of disputes with FIFA. Uruguay stayed away in 1934 because the host country, Italy, had refused to make the trip to South America in 1930. Argentina boycotted the games in 1938, 1950, and 1954 after its bid to host the 1938 tournament was denied. Austria did not compete in 1938 when it temporarily ceased to exist as a state after being invaded by Nazi Germany. India refused to send a team when it first qualified as an independent nation in 1950 after FIFA declared the Indians could not play barefoot, as was their custom. Scotland withdrew from the final rounds of the tournament in 1950 because it had lost to England in earlier rounds and didn't want to enter competition as a runner-up. The Soviet Union boycotted a two-game qualifying playoff in 1974 because it was to be played in Santiago's National Stadium, infamous for housing political prisoners of Augusto Pinochet Ugarte, who had recently overthrown Marxist president Salvador Allende Gossens. Still, the inevitable entry of politics into a championship between nations has ultimately not affected the beauty and excitement of the World Cup.

Originally, the name "football" referred to any game played on foot rather than horseback. This is part of the reason many of the elite looked down on the game: They preferred equestrian sports.

THE UNITED STATES IN THE WORLD CUP

Although the U.S. men's team has rarely been a major World Cup contender, there have been definite highlights over the years for American fans. One of the most memorable came in 1950 when the U.S. team won a "miracle match" over the much-favored English team, 1–0. Like the 1980 U.S. hockey team victory over the USSR, this was the David and Goliath story of its day. The win was front page news in the United Kingdom and in much of Europe, but according to *Soccer's Most Wanted, The New York Times* wedged the story in its sports section next to the St. Louis Browns–Washington Senators baseball score.

More recently, American soccer fans got great news in 1988 when FIFA, looking to tap the enormous American consumer market, gave the nod for the 1994 World Cup to be played in the United States. There were protests around the world from those who wondered

Goalkeeper Frank Borghi is carried aloft by his teammates after the United States upsets England 1–0 in the 1950 World Cup. *Courtesy of the National Soccer Hall of Fame.*

about the wisdom of planning a World Cup in a nation whose team had failed to even qualify for a World Cup in nearly thirty years. But the bar was set, and in 1990, the United States did indeed qualify. By 1994, the Americans were playing in front of sellout crowds. The success of the 1994 men's event, combined with the fact that the American women had established themselves as among the best in international play, led to the United States being named host for the 1999 Women's World Cup.

Without question, the U.S. women's team has been the major soccer story of recent years. They won the first-ever Women's World Cup in China in 1991 (besting Norway 2–1 in the final). Although Norway took the cup in 1995, the United States won it back again in 1999 on it own turf. Despite the fact that Germany took the next two in a row, winning the tournament in 2003 and 2007, the U.S. women's team has secured a spot at the top of the soccer world.

In 1958, eight Manchester United players were killed after their England-bound plane crashed just after takeoff following a 3–3 draw with Red Star Belgrade in Yugoslavia. The clock outside the club offices at the Old Trafford Stadium was permanently stopped at 3:40, the exact time of the crash.

The first night game played under lights took place in Sheffield, England on October 14, 1878, when two Sheffield Football Association clubs played under floodlights powered by a pair of Siemens dynamo engines, said to give off the same amount of light as eight thousand candles.

KEEP YOUR EYE ON THE PRIZE

Since Italy won the World Cup tournament in 1938, the trophy—the coveted cup itself—remained in that country while play was suspended during World War II. As legend has it, Ottorino Barassi, the Italian vice-president of FIFA, hid the trophy from the Nazis in a shoebox under his bed. Others claim it was Jules Rimet, FIFA president, who had the trophy hidden under *his* bed in France. The less exciting but more likely story is that the trophy rode out the war in a bank vault in Rome.

In 1966, the cup (known as the Jules Rimet trophy since 1946) was stolen from Westminster Abbey in London, where it had been on display prior to the games that summer. A few days later, a black-and-white dog named Pickles, digging for a bone, discovered the trophy in a backyard where it had been buried by a man intending to hold it for ransom.

In 1970, the trophy found a permanent home in Brazil when the team was allowed to keep it after winning the World Cup championship for the third time. Then, in 1983, thieves broke into the offices of the Brazilian Soccer Federation and stole the cup. That trophy was never found.

In 1974, a new trophy of 18-karat solid gold, now known as the FIFA World Cup trophy, was designed by an Italian sculptor. The trophy, which is temporarily kept by the reigning World Cup champ and replaced with a replica when the cup moves on, will be retired in 2038 when the plaque with the winners' names is completely filled.

Milestones in Modern Soccer History

1846

The first standardized football rules are drafted in Rugby, England.

1857

Sheffield, the first British football club north of London, is established.

1862

The Oneida Football Club of Boston, the first organized soccer team in the United States, is founded by Gerrit Smith Miller.

Gerrit Smith Miller at age 18. *Courtesy of the National Soccer Hall of Fame.*

1863

On October 26, representatives from several London public schools meet at the Freemason's Tavern to officially codify the rules of football.

1866

Australian Rules football rules are written. ("Australian Rules" remains a wild, uninhibited soccer variant.)

1867

Organized soccer begins in Scotland when YMCA players form a team, Queen's Park.

1871

Soccer's oldest surviving competition, the FA Cup, is created.

1872

Corner kicks are introduced.

The first international match is played between England and Scotland, ending in a score of 0–0.

1873

The Scottish Football Association is founded.

1876

The Football Association of Wales is founded.

The first U.S. intercollegiate soccer match is played in New Brunswick, New Jersey, between Rutgers and Princeton. (Rutgers wins 6–4.) The game, which looked more like rugby than modern soccer, is also claimed by American football historians as *their* first game.

1878

In Sheffield, England, a soccer match is played at night under lights for the first time.

1880

The Irish Football Association is founded.

1884

The American Football Association is formed in Newark, New Jersey, with the purpose of uniting the numerous Eastern clubs and providing uniformity in the interpretation of the rules.

1885

The United States and Canada play each other in the first international soccer match staged outside the British Isles.

The Gaelic Athletic Association is founded and rules for Gaelic football are written.

Paying players (professionalism) is legalized.

1891

Penalty kicks are introduced.

The Bethlehem Steel team. *Courtesy of the National Soccer Hall of Fame.*

1896

Soccer is played as an exhibition sport between teams from Greece and Denmark in the first modern Olympic Games in Athens.

1904

The Fédération Internationale de Football Association (FIFA) is formed in Paris on May 21. Charter members include France, Belgium, Denmark, the Netherlands, Spain, Sweden, and Switzerland. The International Board, the authority over the rules and their interpretation, continues under the jurisdiction of England, Scotland, Ireland, and Wales, even though they are not yet affiliated with FIFA.

1905

The first South American international game is played between Uruguay and Argentina.

1908

Soccer is played at the Olympics for the first time. England takes the gold.

1910

The first Copa America is held; Argentina wins.

1912

Rule change allows goalkeepers to handle the ball only in their own penalty area.

1913

FIFA becomes a member of the International Board, increasing its influence on the interpretation of rules.

The ten-yards rule is introduced for free kicks.

1914

The United States Football Association (USFA) is incorporated and granted full membership in FIFA at the annual congress in Oslo, Norway, on June 24.

Thomas Cahill, founder of the United States Football Association (which later became U.S. Soccer). *Courtesy of the National Soccer Hall of Fame.*

1919

Bethlehem Steel, on tour in Sweden, becomes the first American professional team to play in Europe.

1920

The Dick-Kerr's Ladies Professional Team tours the United States. They notch a 3–3–2 record and outscore their male opponents 35–34.

1921

The original American Soccer League (ASL) begins play with franchises in Fall River (Mass.), Philadelphia, Jersey City, Brooklyn, New York, Holyoke (Mass.), and Pawtucket (R.I.).

1923

The world's first indoor soccer league debuts at Boston's Commonwealth Calvary Armory.

1926

Legendary Brazilian player Artur Friedenreich marks his one-thousandth goal.

1927

A soccer match (Arsenal vs. Sheffield at Highbury Stadium in London) is broadcast on radio for the first time on January 22.

1930

Thirteen nations compete in the first FIFA World Cup in Montevideo, Uruguay.

1933

The National Collegiate Athletic Association (NCAA), the governing body of college athletics in the United States, releases the official rulebook for intercollegiate soccer.

1938

West Chester State College and Salisbury College play the first intercollegiate soccer game under floodlights.

1938

England's FA Cup final becomes soccer's first live TV broadcast.

1941

The National Soccer Coaches Association of America (NSCAA) is formed.

1945

The USFA changes its name to the United States Soccer Football Association (USSFA).

Walter Bahr, U.S. national team captain, during the 1950 World Cup. *Courtesy of the National Soccer Hall of Fame.*

1950

The United States beats England 1–0 at the World Cup in Brazil, marking the biggest upset ever in international soccer.

The first college bowl game is played in St. Louis on January 1. Penn State ties the University of San Francisco 2–2.

The National Soccer Hall of Fame is founded by the Philadelphia Old-Timers Association with fifteen inaugural inductees.

1959

Pratt Institute defeats Elizabethtown College 4–3 in

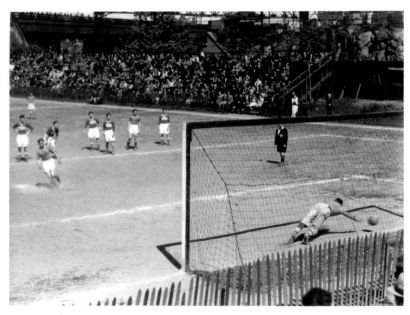

Penalty kick at Starlight Park, circa 1940. *Courtesy of the National Soccer Hall of Fame.*

the first National Association of Intercollegiate Athletics college championship in Slippery Rock, Pennsylvania.

St. Louis University defeats Bridgeport University 5–2 in the first NCAA championship tournament in Storrs, Connecticut.

1960

The International Soccer League (ISL), composed of top-rated European, British, and South American teams, begins play under the sponsorship of the ASL. For more than a decade, foreign teams will visit the United States to play American teams.

1961

The Confederation of North, Central American and Caribbean Association Football (CONCACAF), the successor of the Central American and Caribbean Confederation, is formed on September 18 in Mexico City.

1967

Two new major professional leagues debut in the United States: the USSFA-sanctioned United Soccer Association (USA) and the independent National Professional Soccer League (NPSL). The leagues soon merge to form the North American Soccer League (NASL).

The first Hermann Trophy for college player of the year is awarded to Dov Markus of Long Island University.

1971

Pelé plays his last game (Brazil ties Yugoslavia 2–2) before 150,000 spectators at Rio de Janiero's Maracana Stadium and retires from international competition.

1972

Title IX of the Omnibus Education Act is passed. It will effectively change women's soccer (and all women's sports) in America over the next generation.

1974

The USSFA changes its name to the United States Soccer Federation (USSF).

The NASL reaches a membership of eighteen teams.

American soccer star Kyle Rote, Jr., wins the first of his three victories on ABC-TV Superstars competitions against elite athletes from other major sports.

1975

In April, the New York Cosmos sign Pelé for a reported $4.5 million.

1977

The NASL signs a seven-game national TV contract.

On October 1, in his farewell game at Giants Stadium, Pelé plays for both sides (the New York Cosmos and FC Santos, his former team from Brazil) in front of a crowd of 77,202.

1978

The Major Indoor Soccer League (MISL) debuts with six franchises: Cincinnati Kids, Cleveland Force, Houston Summit, New York Arrows, Philadelphia Fever, and Pittsburgh Spirit.

1982

The MISL season opens with fourteen teams, including three NASL teams participating for a season (San Jose, Chicago, and San Diego).

The National Soccer Hall of Fame and Museum opens in Oneonta, NY.

1984

Four NASL teams permanently join the MISL (New York, Chicago, San Diego, and Minnesota).

The ASL cancels what would have been its fiftieth season.

Both the American Indoor Soccer Association (AISA) and the United Soccer League (USL) are formed.

1985

The first U.S. Women's National Team competes in Italy.

The North American Soccer League and the United Soccer League both fold.

1986

The Western Soccer Alliance (WSA) debuts with seven teams.

1988

The ASL resumes play with ten teams.

On July 4, during the FIFA Congress in Zurich, the United States is awarded the hosting of the 1994 World Cup.

1989

The inaugural FIFA World Championship is played in the Netherlands.

The World Cup was broadcast on TV for the first time in 1954. (Yugoslavia beat France 1–0.)

1990

U.S. Men's National Team competes in the World Cup for the first time in forty years.

The WSL and the ASL merge to form the American Professional Soccer League.

1991

The U.S. Women's National Team beats Norway (2–1) to win the first-ever FIFA Women's World Championship on November 30.

The United States Under-23 team wins gold at the Pan Am Games in Cuba.

1992

The U.S. Men's National Team wins the inaugural U.S. Cup 1992 in June.

The Major Indoor Soccer League folds after fifteen years in existence.

1996

The U.S. Women's National Team wins the first gold medal ever awarded in women's soccer after defeating China 2–1 in the championship game at the Olympics in Atlanta.

Major League Soccer kicks off and averages more than 17,000 fans per game during its first season.

In the early years of the World Cup, teams that scored the first goal in the finals were said to be jinxed because they rarely won. The "curse" was broken in the early 1970s.

1997

The Continental Indoor Soccer League ceases operations after five seasons.

1999

The United States Women's National Team wins the 1999 Women's World Cup by defeating China 5–4 in overtime.

The Under-18 Women's National Team captures the gold medal at the Pan American Games in Winnipeg.

2000

Norway defeats the U.S. Women in overtime to win the gold at the Sydney Olympics. The U.S. Men take fourth place, their highest Olympic finish to date.

2001

The Women's United Soccer Association (WUSA) begins play, with the Bay Area CyberRays winning the inaugural Founders Cup.

Mia Hamm is named the first-ever FIFA Women's World Player of the Year.

The National Professional Soccer League, in existence since 1984, merges with the WISL and is renamed the Major Indoor Soccer League.

2002

The U.S. Men win the CONCACAF Gold Cup in January with a 2–0 victory over Costa Rica for the first Gold Cup title for the United States since 1991. The U.S. Women also capture the gold.

2003

After the outbreak of Severe Acute Respiratory Syndrome (SARS), FIFA relocates the Women's World Cup from China to the United States. Germany takes the gold.

2004

The U. S. Women's National Team wins every tournament it enters, culminating with the 2004 Olympics in Athens.

2007

In July, British superstar David Beckham signs with the L. A. Galaxy.

2008

The U.S. Women beat Denmark (2–1) to win the Algarve Cup for the fifth time in the previous six years.

At the Beijing Olympics, the gold medals go to Argentina (men's team) and the United States (women's team).

2009

The Seattle Sounders begin play as an MLS franchise.

In 1998, the World Cup eliminated the full thirty minutes of overtime and replaced it with a sudden death or "golden goal" format. The first golden goal in history was scored in the second round by Laurent Blanc of France in his team's 1–0 victory over Paraguay.

3: THE RIGHT STUFF

Getting Equipped for Soccer

Over the years, soccer has often been referred to as the Simplest Game. This nickname refers partly to the simple objective: Kick (or head) the ball into the goal to score. But no doubt the moniker also refers to the very short list of absolutely necessary game items: shoes and a ball.

Sure, when we make it FIFA official, there are a few more necessities: uniforms, regulation goals, cleats, shin guards, goalie gloves, and cards and flags for the referees. But the fact that the equipment is so basic makes this game accessible to any player anywhere in the world.

WHAT TO WEAR

According to the *Laws of the Game:*

Safety: *A player must not use equipment or wear anything which is dangerous to himself or another player (including any kind of jewelry).*

Basic Equipment: *The basic compulsory equipment of a player comprises the following separate items:*

Dressed for action.

- *a jersey or shirt—if undergarments are worn, the color of the sleeve should be the same main color as the sleeve of the jersey or shirt;*
- *shorts—if undershorts are worn, they are of the same main color as the shorts;*
- *stockings;*
- *shinguards;*
- *footwear*

Shinguards:

- *are covered entirely by the stockings*
- *are made of a suitable material (rubber, plastic, or similar substances)*
- *provide a reasonable degree of protection*

Goalkeepers:

- *each goalkeeper wears colors which distinguish him from the other players, the referee and the assistant referees*

GAME DAY

Player's equipment list:

- Sports bag to carry all personal items

- Water jug (the bigger the better)

- Soccer shoes

- Shin guards

- Sock straps

- Uniform socks

- Uniform jersey

- Plastic bag to protect soccer bag in case of rain

- Personal first-aid items (band aids, athletic tape, etc.)

Gearing up for game time.

Note: Many coaches ask their team to wear uniform shorts, a warm-up t-shirt, and flats or exercise sandals to the field on game day. The players change into their uniform jerseys and soccer shoes and put on their socks, sock straps, and shin guards just prior to game time.

FEET FIRST

In order to develop great soccer feet, a player needs just the right pair of shoes. Soccer shoes, or "boots," as they say in the United Kingdom, are a player's most important tool. Indoor shoes or "flats" are different from outdoor shoes to accommodate the difference in playing surface. Although kids kicking a ball around in a neighborhood pick-up game may wear any shoes they like, wearing running shoes or other athletic shoes on the soccer field is discouraged and even against the rules in some leagues.

Like most athletic shoes, soccer shoes have come a long way in terms of materials and technology.

Gotta get good feet.

Until the 1940s, most playing shoes were made from thick, non-waterproofed leather that became really heavy, not to mention unwieldy, on a wet field. Today, the world's top players seek out shoes with microfiber uppers, to keep the foot dry, and look for components such as carbon-fiber footplates and lace covers, which may provide an edge in contact with the ball.

Shoes or cleats come in every imaginable color these days, but black is probably the most popular color for players worldwide. Some clubs have rules about the color of shoes to be worn, since the shoes are part of the uniform. Ditto for socks and the stretchy sock straps that go on top and hold the socks and shin guards in place.

A comfortable fit is the most important consideration when choosing a shoe. Both indoor and outdoor shoes are usually a half size smaller than an athlete's running shoes to allow for an accurate touch on the ball. Shoes that are too big can cause blisters and make a player miserable!

The kicker: Today's shoes are light and sleek.

Boot up.

Outdoor Soccer Shoes

Specific requirements vary from league to league, but most players wear shoes with cleats or studs. Keep in mind the field conditions you will most likely encounter. (Your coach can help you with this.)

Turf shoes, equipped with dozens of small rubber studs on the outsole to provide traction and absorb shock to your feet, are best for artificial surfaces or on hard, compacted fields.

Firm ground shoes, equipped with twelve medium-length studs or blades, are good all-around footwear that work well on soft and hard fields.

Soft ground shoes, equipped with replaceable studs or with a bladed outsole, are made for soft field conditions. They're worn mostly by players 14 years old and older.

She'll grow out of them before she wears them out.

Indoor Soccer Shoes

Also known as "flats," indoor shoes are very similar to regular running shoes. They have no cleats or studs, but they differ from regular sneakers since they usually have soccer shoe uppers.

Tip for Parents: Many players outgrow shoes before they are worn out. Get together with other parents (or have the kids get together) to swap shoes before investing in brand new ones. When buying new shoes, try to buy a good but moderately priced pair that best matches your player's anticipated field conditions. Note: For the price of one pair of high-end shoes, you can buy three pairs and be ready for all conditions. If you can afford only one pair, it's probably best to buy firm ground shoes.

SHIN GUARDS

If there is one piece of equipment that a soccer player appreciates, it's his trusty pair of shin guards. Although a soccer mom with three players under the age of six may curse the pads as she struggles to slip them on her aspiring young Pelés every Saturday, protecting the shins from dozens of inevitable kicks during every match and practice is an absolute necessity.

The first shin guards, invented in 1874 by Samuel W. Widdowson who played for Nottingham Forest and later for England, were big and brown and fastened around the shin with long ribbons. Today, most shin guards are pretty sleek and are held in place with Velcro closures. Younger players should look for comfortable lightweight pads. More advanced players should try shin guards with molded shells for better performance.

Shin guards: Don't leave home without them. Snug but not too tight.

Keeping the pads in place is essential. Most shin guards come with straps. Even so, it's not unusual to see an occasional midfielder securing the pads with athletic tape. Some players go an extra step and buy compression sleeves, elastic tubes that slip over the lower leg—shin guard and all—and hold the guards firmly in place.

England's Nottingham Forest Club is credited with introducing shin guards, the goalpost crossbar, goal netting, and the referee's whistle, all in the late 1870s.

SHIN GUARDS TIPS

- Shin guards should be lightweight and fit snugly but comfortably.
- Always wear shin guards under the socks, not over them.
- Shin guards should extend from just below the knee to two or three inches above the ankle.
- Consider shin guards with ankle padding attached (these stay in place really well thanks to the stirrup in the pad). You can also buy separate padded ankle guards.

UNIFORMS

During the Victorian era, the typical outfit for a soccer player consisted of a cap, a button-down shirt often made of thick, scratchy wool, and knee breeches. Today's players are clad in functional, breathable cotton or microfiber shorts and jerseys.

On game day, teams show their colors.

In soccer, the jersey gets all the glamour. National team players from around the world have a tradition of trading jerseys with opponents after big matches. Famous players often simply give their jerseys away. (It's estimated that Pelé gave away over twenty thousand shirts in his career.)

Soccer players have also become known for taking off their shirts in celebration. One of the most iconic images in sports is the U.S. Women's Brandi Chastain whipping off her jersey following her winning penalty kick at the 1999 Women's World Cup, effectively putting the sports bra on the map.

Keepers should stand out.

Obviously, jerseys vary from team to team. Most clubs have different jerseys for home games, away games, and practice, and all players wear the same outfits, except for the goalkeeper.

Keeper Kits

In order for the goalkeeper to stand out from other players, as well as from the referees, she wears a different-colored jersey than her teammates. Until the 1980s, the rules stated that goalies could wear only green, yellow, or white. Today, just about anything goes, and keepers often get creative wearing neon colors and patterns (one design featured an archery target!) on the theory that opponents who can see the goalie will kick the ball right to her, enabling her to make the save.

Note: Many coaches encourage keepers to wear jerseys with elbow and forearm padding attached. Also, many keepers forgo shorts and wear pants with pads (sliders), especially on cold days or when playing on particularly rough fields.

GOALIE GLOVES

Young goalies (under 11) don't always play with gloves. This will be the coach's call. Still, it's a good idea for the coach to keep a couple of pairs on hand for players trying out the position. Once players advance, they shoot harder, so a keeper will want to buy her own pair of gloves to protect her hands and make it easier to grip and save the ball.

Players and their parents will need to decide how much of an investment to make. Expensive gloves with smooth palms made of thick, soft, spongy white latex foam provide excellent grip and shock absorption but wear out relatively quickly. Gloves with textured palms last a little longer and cost less.

Overall, the most important factor is comfort.

Soccer was introduced to Russia in the late 1800s by two Englishmen, the Charnock brothers, who ran a mill outside Moscow. Lacking money for boots (shoes), they asked a strap piercer at the mill to attach studs to the players' regular work shoes. Problem solved.

GOALIE GLOVE TIPS

- Consider buying two pairs of gloves, one for games and one for practice.
- Purchase gloves with plenty of room for your fingers to move, usually one size bigger than a snug fit.

HATS OFF

When a broadcaster says, "Beckham earned his one-hundredth cap for England this year," this means that Becks played in his one-hundredth game for the English national team. In fact, soccer players don't wear caps, though they used to way back when. Before team shirts were first worn (during the first international game between England and Scotland in 1872), caps were what distinguished one team from another. In fact, caps were the uniforms. Somewhere along the line, soccer players ditched the caps (all the better to head the ball?), and today, if a player is actually handed a cap, it's a treasured keepsake.

Hands! Goalies cover them up.

FIELD GEAR

BALLS

Throughout history, soccer balls have been made of a variety of materials, such as coconuts, pig bladders, and even, legend has it, the severed heads of conquered enemies. Throughout the nineteenth and early twentieth centuries, balls were often made of the same materials used to make shoes: heavy, non-waterproofed leather. Add a little bit of rain or mud to this equation and the balls became sodden and often unmanageable.

These days, most balls are made of plastic or synthetic leather. Young players usually play with the plastic balls, while more advanced players usually use hand-stitched synthetics.

Traditionally, soccer balls have thirty-two panels, although some high-tech models have as few as six panels to cut down on the wind resistance the stitching creates. The most popular soccer balls are made of a latex rubber core covered with polyurethane. The most expensive balls are covered with several layers of polyurethane, which makes them super-soft. Most youth soccer players will do well with a single-layered ball. Whatever kind you choose, you will probably need a pump to keep your ball properly inflated.

A soccer player's tool kit begins with a good ball.

According to the *Laws of the Game:*

The ball is:

- *spherical*
- *made of leather or other suitable material*
- *of a circumference of not more than 70 cm (28 ins) and not less than 68 cm (27 ins)*
- *not more than 450 g (16 oz) in weight and not less than 410 g (14 oz) at the start of the match*
- *of a pressure equal to 0.6–1.1 atmosphere (600–1100 g/cm2) at sea level (8.5 lbs/sq in–15.6 lbs/sq in)*

Heavy-duty shoes and ball, circa 1920.

The ball specifications listed in the *Laws of the Game* are for size 5 balls, designed for players age 12 and older. Youth players are permitted to (and should) play with smaller balls. Beginners sometimes play with balls as small as sizes 1 and 2, which are also called "mini" or "skill" balls. For matches, players should play with the following sizes:

AGE	SIZE
4–7	3*
8–11	4**
12 and up	5

* Circumference 23–24 inches (58–61 cm), weight 11–12 ounces (312–340 gm).
** Circumference 25–26 inches (64–66 cm), weight 11–14 ounces (312–397 gm).

Got a ball? Got a game!

Most teams count a bag of training balls as part of their equipment list. It's traditional for players to take turns taking the bag home after practice or games and being responsible for the bag. When your turn comes up, be sure the balls are all properly inflated when you bring them to the next training session or game.

GRAY GHOSTS

A coach may want to think twice before choosing gray for her team's uniforms. In 1996, Manchester United played the first half of a game in special gray uniforms. (Replicas were sold in stores by the thousands.) The coach blamed the color of the jerseys on the team's poor performance (3–0) at halftime, pointing out the players had difficulty seeing each other on the field. They switched back to blue, white, and yellow jerseys for the remainder of the game.—*Soccer's Most Wanted*

TIP FOR PLAYERS

Every soccer player should have his own ball. At least one. This way he can practice at home.

PELÉ MELÉE

Since every fan and player wanted to "trade" shirts with Pelé, his Santos team used to bring as many as one hundred of his numbered jerseys with them on the road. When Pelé was mobbed by fans who wanted to take his actual shirt, he would often take it off and throw it far away so he could escape unscathed.

Have balls, will travel.

Players set their goals.

Smart. Very smart. If there is no referee on hand to tally a score, players may want to use a new piece of equipment known as an "intelligent ball," which transmits a signal when it crosses a wired goal line.

GOALS

These days, soccer goals are a familiar sight on playing fields at parks and schools just about everywhere. Especially on game day, the goal is fixed and in place well in advance. Still, many coaches invest in a set of portable goals to keep in the car and bring to practice. This is a great idea if the coach finds her team at a field without goals or if she wants to set up extra goals for shooting drills.

Players may also want to invest in their own portable goal to set up at home. Small bounce-backs or rebounders, fabric attachments stretched tight across the front of the goal to automatically return the ball to the kicker, are a terrific way for kids to practice by themselves.

ADDITIONAL EQUIPMENT

Coaches will also want to keep a few extra supplies on hand for practices and games. Round out the gear list with:

- A pump (to inflate balls)
- Traffic cones (to use for drills or as makeshift goals)
- A first-aid kit
- A set of scrimmage vests or pinnies
- Water (several gallon containers and plastic cups)

4: Just for Kicks

How to Play the Beautiful Game

Take a foot, a ball, and something that can pass for a goal and you've got soccer. Hence the nickname: the Simplest Game.

There are seventeen rules, also known as the *Laws of the Game,* and they have barely changed since they were put to paper in 1863. They are universal. Whether you're playing in Buenos Aires, Bangkok, or Barcelona, the rules remain the same. Women and men play by the same rules. World Cup contenders play by the same rules. High-school kids across America play by the same rules. With a little flexibility thrown in for younger or less experienced players, soccer players everywhere play an identical game.

PLAY BY THE RULES

No matter who is playing or where the match takes place, the objective remains the same: Put the ball into the opposing goal using your feet, head, or any other body part except for your arms or hands. The team that does this the most times wins.

It's that simple.

THE FIELD

The *Laws of the Game* outline the following field specifications:

Field Surface:

■ *Matches may be played on natural or artificial surfaces, according to the rules of the competition.*

Dimensions:

■ *The field of play must be rectangular. The length of the touch line must be greater than the length of the goal line.*

■ *Length: minimum 90 m (100 yards)*
maximum 120 m (130 yards)

■ *Width: minimum 45 m (50 yards)*
maximum 90 m (100 yards)

International Matches:

■ *Length: minimum 100 m (110 yards)*
maximum 110 m (120 yards)

- Width: minimum 64 m (70 yards)

  maximum 75 m (80 yards)

Field Markings:

- The field of play is marked with lines. These lines belong to the areas of which they are boundaries.
- The two longer boundary lines are called touch lines. The two shorter lines are called goal lines.
- All lines are not more than 12cm (5ins) wide.
- The field of play is divided into two halves by a halfway line.
- The center mark is indicated at the midpoint of the halfway line. A circle with a radius of 9.15 m (10 yards) is marked around it.

The Goal Area:

- A goal area is defined at each end of the field as follows:
- Two lines are drawn at right angles to the goal line, 5.5 m (6 yards) from the inside of each goalpost. These lines extend into the field of play for a distance of 5.5 m (6 yards) and are joined by a line drawn parallel with the goal line. The area bounded by these lines and the goal line is the goal area.

The Penalty Area:

- A penalty area is defined at each end of the field as follows:

  Two lines are drawn at right angles to the goal line, 16.5 m (18 yards) from the inside of each goalpost. These lines extend into the field of play for a distance of 16.5 m (18 yards) and are joined by a line drawn parallel with the goal line. The area bounded by these lines and the goal line is the penalty area.

  Within each penalty area a penalty mark is made 11 m (12 yards) from the midpoint between the goalposts and equidistant to them. An arc of a circle with a radius of 9.15 m (10 yards) from each penalty mark is drawn outside the penalty area.

- *A flagpost, not less than 1.5 m (5 ft) high, with a non-pointed top and a flag is placed at each corner.*
- *Flagposts may also be placed at each end of the halfway line, not less than 1 m (1 yd) outside the touch line.*

The Corner Arc:

- *A quarter circle with a radius of 1 m (1 yd) from each corner flagpost is drawn inside the field of play.*

Goals:

- *Goals must be placed on the center of each goal line.*
- *They consist of two upright posts equidistant from the corner flagposts and joined at the top by a horizontal crossbar.*
- *The distance between the posts is 7.32 m (8 yds) and the distance from the lower edge of the crossbar to the ground is 2.44 m (8 ft).*
- *Both goalposts and the crossbar have the same width and depth which do not exceed 12 cm (5 ins). The goal lines are the same width as that of the goalposts and the crossbar. Nets may be attached to the goals and the ground behind the goal, provided that they are properly supported and do not interfere with the goalkeeper.*
- *The goalposts and crossbars must be white.*

The Field of Play

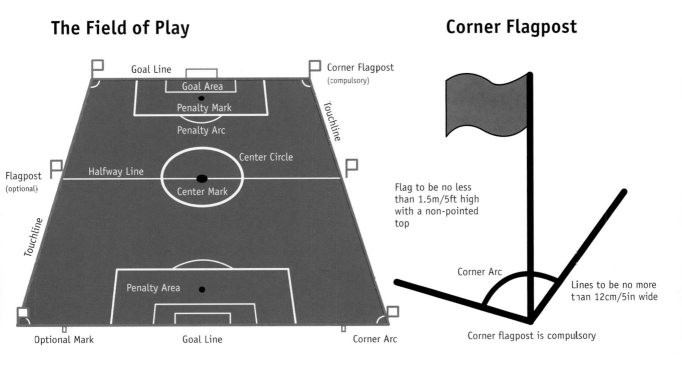

Corner Flagpost

Corner Flagpost (compulsory)

Goal Line

Goal Area

Penalty Mark

Penalty Arc

Touchline

Center Circle

Flagpost (optional)

Halfway Line

Center Mark

Touchline

Penalty Area

Optional Mark

Goal Line

Corner Arc

Flag to be no less than 1.5m/5ft high with a non-pointed top

Corner Arc

Lines to be no more than 12cm/5in wide

Corner flagpost is compulsory

Field Measurements

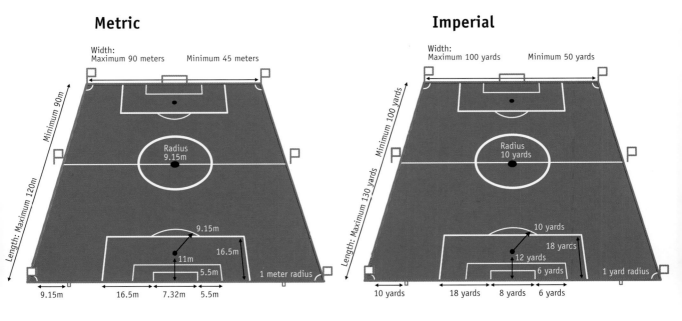

Metric

Width:
Maximum 90 meters   Minimum 45 meters

Minimum 90m

Radius 9.15m

Length: Maximum 120m

9.15m

11m

16.5m

5.5m

9.15m

16.5m

7.32m

5.5m

1 meter radius

Imperial

Width:
Maximum 100 yards   Minimum 50 yards

Minimum 100 yards

Radius 10 yards

Length: Maximum 130 yards

10 yards

18 yards

12 yards

6 yards

10 yards

18 yards

8 yards

6 yards

1 yard radius

NUMBER OF PLAYERS

A soccer match is played by two teams consisting of eleven players each, including the goalkeeper. (Exception: Some youth teams use fewer players. See "Youth Notes" on page 82.) A match may not start if either team has fewer than seven players on the field. Up to three substitutions may be made during the match (up to six in top-level national team matches). A substitute may enter the playing field (from the halfway line, during a stoppage in play) only after receiving a signal from the official. A player who has been replaced takes no further part in the match.

Note: Any other player may change places with the goalkeeper provided that the referee is informed prior to the change and the substitution is made during a stoppage in play.

Players take the field.

In Norway, matches in the northern part of the country are played some two hundred miles above the Arctic Circle where the sun shines all day and all night, so even night games are played with no lights.

TIME

The match lasts for two equal periods of forty-five minutes, unless otherwise agreed by both teams and the referee before the start of play. (For example, teams might agree to play forty-minute halves if the light is fading). Players are entitled to a halftime break of no more than fifteen minutes. The referee allows for time lost due to substitutions, injuries, or any other cause. Additional time is allotted for a penalty kick to be taken at the end of each half.

WHY SOCCER?

"It's such a fast-paced game. You have to be aware at all times and be a quick thinker. Anything can happen in soccer—the worst team car beat the best team! It happens all the time. It brings people from different backgrounds together. I am only one of four Caucasian kids on my team; all the rest are Hispanic. We are a tight group that works well together. Without soccer our paths might never have crossed."—*Alex Carr, age 18, Fallbrook, California*

YOUTH NOTES

Although the *Laws of the Game* were written with all ages in mind, youth leagues have a great deal of leeway in making adjustments in field size, number of players, and so on to suit the ages and experience levels of their teams. U.S. Youth Soccer provides the following guidelines:

AGE	FIELD DIMENSIONS	PLAYERS PER TEAM	GAME LENGTH (IN MINUTES)
U-6	25 x 20 yds (22.9 x 18.3 m)	3	32
U-8	50 x 30 yds (48.7 x 27.4 m)	4	48
U-10	70 x 50 yds (64.0 x 45.7 m)	8	50
U-12	100 x 50 yds (91.4 x 45.7 m)	11	60
U-14	100 x 50 yds (91.4 x 45.7 m)	11	70
U-16	100 x 50 yds (91.4 x 45.7 m)	11	80
U-19	100 x 50 yds (91.4 x 45.7 m)	11	90

Note: The field dimensions are the minimum required; fields may be larger.

Goalkeepers are not usually used in Under-6 and Under-8 play, and a keeper is optional in Under-10. For youth players, the *Laws of the Game* also provide for adjustments to the goal, specifically in the width between the goalposts and the height of the crossbar from the ground, and for the number of substitutions (it varies by age, but more are allowed in the youth game).

In youth soccer, everybody wins.

START AND RESTART OF PLAY

Matches are started and restarted by way of a kickoff, dropped ball, throw-in, goal kick, or corner kick.

Kickoff

The match begins with a coin toss, after which the winner chooses which goal to attack during the first half of the game. The opposing team then takes the kickoff to start the game. (The team that won the toss takes the kickoff to start the second half of the match, when the teams also switch goals.) Kickoffs are also used to restart play after a team scores a goal.

Note: A goal may be scored directly from the kickoff.

Dropped Ball

Following a temporary stop in play, a match is restarted with a dropped ball: The referee drops the ball at the exact spot where the play was stopped. When the ball touches the ground, play resumes.

Throw-Ins

A match may be restarted by way of a throw-in after the ball crosses the touchline on the ground or in the air. The team opposing the player who last touched the ball takes the throw-in from the point where it crossed the touchline; a player stands behind the touchline and throws the ball with both hands from behind his head. The ball is in play the moment it enters the field of play. The thrower may not touch the ball again until it has touched another player.

Note: A goal may not be scored directly from a throw-in.

Goal Kicks

A match may be restarted by way of a goal kick after the ball, last touched by the attacking team, crosses the goal line on the ground or in the air. A defending player kicks the ball from any point within the goal area. All members of the opposing team must remain outside the penalty area until the ball is beyond the penalty area and back in play. The kicker may not play the ball again until another player touches it first.

Note: a goal may be scored directly from a goal kick.

Corner Kicks

A match may be restarted with a corner kick when the ball, last touched by the defending team, crosses the goal line on the ground or in the air. An attacking player kicks the ball from inside the nearest corner arc. All members of the opposing team must remain at least 10 yards (9.1 m) from the ball until it is in play. The kicker may not play the ball again until another player touches it.

Note: A goal may be scored directly from a corner kick.

In and Out

The ball is out of play after it has entirely crossed the goal line or

In bounds.

Out of bounds.

touchline on the ground or in the air or when the referee has stopped play. The ball is in play at all other times. Remember, the line itself is part of the field of play, so a ball on the line is in bounds.

Onside

Whether it's during a restart or a drive toward the goal, players must remain "onside" at all times. In soccer, a player is called "offside" if she is nearer to her opponent's goal than both the ball and the second-to-last opponent while the ball is being played. The official will only call "offside" if the player has interfered with play or with an opponent or if her team gains an advantage by her taking that position. (More on this rule in Chapter 8.)

AIN'T MISBEHAVIN'

Soccer is not a contact sport. But inevitably, contact occurs. It's up to the referee to decide if the contact was appropriate and if no harm was intended. As a rule, a player may not kick, trip, charge, jump at, strike, or hold an opponent. Further, a player may not perform in a dangerous way, obstruct an opponent, or stop the goalkeeper from releasing the ball from his hands. If he does any of these things, the referee will call a penalty.

GOAL!

A goal is scored when the entire ball crosses the line between the goalposts. The team that scores the most goals wins. If both teams score an equal number of goals, the match is a draw. Depending on the league and level of play, sometimes teams play overtime to break ties. In high-level cup competitions, tied matches are often decided by a series of penalty kicks. Usually, teams take five kicks apiece. If the score is still tied at that point, teams will go into sudden death, where the teams take turns taking one kick at a time until one side scores.

Since World Cup rules require games to be played on grass fields, Michigan's Pontiac Silverdome faced a problem when the indoor venue was selected to host a World Cup final. So, a field of perennial rye and Kentucky bluegrass was grown in the parking lot and laid on top of the turf. (Cost: $2.4 million.)

Why Soccer?

"I like it because of the contact, using your feet, and because soccer is just overall fun! I like getting outside and playing in the mud. I would rather be a soccer player than a cheerleader. This way, people are cheering for me!"—Anne Baumhower, age 13, Fairhope, Alabama

Indoor Rules

Rules vary from league to league, but indoor soccer deviates from outdoor (a.k.a. standard) soccer in some nearly universal respects:

The field: Most indoor soccer arenas are rectangular or oblong in shape, with artificial turf floors. In many collegiate intramural leagues, the game may be played on basketball courts. Walls at least six feet tall bound the arena. Ceiling heights vary. Arenas are generally smaller than standard soccer fields—commonly 200 feet by 85 feet (61.0 m by 26.0 m), the regulation size for a hockey rink in North America—and the goals are recessed into the walls. Goals are also smaller than in standard soccer, and generally the penalty area is smaller too.

The team: Most indoor soccer games are played with six active players per team, one of whom is the goalkeeper. Substitute players are permitted.

Play off of walls: The ball may be struck in such a way that it contacts one or more walls without penalty or stoppage. If the ball flies over a wall or contacts the ceiling, play is stopped and the team opposing the one that most recently touched the ball is awarded a free kick at the location where the ball left the arena or made contact with the ceiling.

Contact: Standard contact rules generally apply (ball contact must be made during a play on the ball, no charging with hands or elbows, no charging from behind, etc). Many leagues ban the use of the sliding tackle, a technique that's less useful on turf or wood than it is on a slick field anyway.

No offside: Most leagues play without an offside rule.

GET IN POSITION

There are four basic positions in soccer: goalkeeper, defender, midfielder, and forward. Players are assigned specific duties, but since soccer is a game of ebbs and flows, every position adopts the responsibilities of another position at some point during a game.

So, it's not unusual to see a forward defending, a defender attacking, or even a goalie dribbling, passing, or (it's rare but it happens) scoring! The Beautiful Game is full of surprises. That said, here is the breakdown of positions and the player's job in each.

Keepers use everything they've got to protect the net.

GOALKEEPER

What?

Protects the goal.

Where?

Technically, she can be anywhere on the field, but straying too far from the goal is not recommended, for obvious reasons. Most keepers stick mainly to the middle and front part of the goal area except when their team is clustered around the opposite goal working toward notching a score.

Got reach?

How?

The keeper uses her body, hands, feet, and head to deflect attempted scores. The keeper is the only player allowed to use her hands on the field, although she must remain within the 18-by-44-yard (16.46-by-40.23-meter) penalty area to do so. (If she handles the ball outside the box, the other team is awarded a penalty kick.)

WHY SOCCER?

"Kicking!"—*Adam Hamburg, age 6, Waconia, Minnesota*

Who?

Fearless players and natural-born leaders make great goalies. They should be alert, quick, and thick-skinned. (All eyes are on the keeper, who shoulders the responsibility when the other team scores.) A little extra height or an explosive ability to jump is a plus.

Bonus

The goalkeeper often plays the role of on-field coach, cheering for her teammates and calling out instructions from her downfield vantage point.

DEFENDER

What?

Stops or slows down attacks by the opposing team.

On "D," players go for the ball.

Where?

In front of the goalkeeper, mostly in the defensive third of the field.

How?

A defender attempts to keep opposing players (and the ball) far from his team's goal by patrolling the flanks and center of the field. His most successful plays involve stealing the ball from an attacker and passing it far downfield and out of harm's way.

Why Soccer?

"I love it because of the feeling I get after I score a goal!"—Brady Kucharski, age 10, Westminster, Maryland

Who?

Most teams assign four defenders. Attack-minded coaches may use only three; more conservative skippers will employ five or even (rarely) six. There are two kinds of defenders: outside fullbacks, who work the right and left edges of the field, and central defenders, who cover the middle of the defensive area, playing either side by side or in a sweeper-stopper combination with one player positioned in front of the other.

The best defenders are team-oriented players who are flexible enough to shift between different defensive strategies during the course of the match.

Bonus

It's not unusual for defenders to take part in the attack (for example, when a fullback runs forward on the left or right flank into the attacking half). Coaches call this overlapping.

MIDFIELDER

What?

Serves as the link between attack and defense.

Making the transition.

Where?

Usually positioned in the middle third of the field, between the defenders and the forwards.

How?

A player in this position uses ball handling and passing to control the midfield. She attempts to pick off the other team's passes and transitions the ball from defense to offense.

Who?

Coaches generally call on four midfielders (also sometimes called "linkmen"), although the number can vary from three to six. There are two classifications: defensive (or stay-at-home) midfielders and attacking midfielders. Strong runners are the best athletes for this position.

Bonus

Midfielders who play both an attacking and a defensive role are sometimes called "two-way midfielders." These are versatile players (often energetic team leaders) charged with organizing the midfield area.

FORWARD

What?

Takes most of the shots on goal. His job is to score.

Where?

Either the middle or the side of the field, covering the entire pitch but ideally finding himself near the opposing goal.

How?

When opportunity knocks, forwards must be ready to pounce on a loose ball, gain control of it, and shoot to score.

Who?

Forwards tend to be either strikers (also called "center forwards"), who play the middle and farthest forward, or wings, who work the right and left flanks and either shoot from the penalty areas or set up shots for the striker.

Bonus

The striker should be a team's most dangerous (that is, best-shooting) player. This is a glamorous position—but when he fails to score, a striker takes the heat.

Forward roll!

X'S AND O'S

A coach has a choice in the formation—the tactical set-up—he uses for his team. (For the most part, young players stay away from complicated formations during games.) The common formations below list just ten players, because the goalkeeper is a constant in every formation.

4-5-1: 4 defenders, 5 midfielders, and 1 forward. (Used most often by pros.)

4-4-2: 4 defenders, 4 midfielders, and 2 forwards. (Probably the most common formation.)

4-3-3: 4 defenders, 3 midfielders, and 3 forwards on the field. (Considered a more defensive formation.)

4-2-4: 4 defenders, 2 midfielders, and 4 forwards. (Considered the most offense-minded formation.)

WHAT'S YOUR COVERAGE?

In soccer, positions aren't as strict as they are in sports such as baseball or football. Players' roles continually shift from the moment the ball is in play. It's helpful for coaches of young or beginning players to teach positions as a starting point, emphasizing that after the kickoff, everybody scrambles and adjusts to the positions where they can best serve their team. Some coaches use a diagram or chalkboard to demonstrate positions at first. It's also a good idea (during practice) for coaches to physically place players on the field according to their position.

Position? What position?

A great exercise to try: Have players get in position. Kick a ball onto the field and have players play it for a minute or so. Blow the whistle. Have players stop, look at where they are, then return to the starting position. Engage the players in a discussion of where they ended up and how that helped the team.

COVERAGE TIP

Many coaches advise young athletes to play as many positions as possible. Since there is a great deal of overlap in skills required this is not an out of reach goal. Experience on all parts of the field is incredibly valuable as players develop and advance in the game.

MY BEST GAME

"When my team won back-to-back county and tournament championships after being told we couldn't do it. Players from other teams said we didn't have a shot because we had lost one of our top scorers from the year before. Then, we did it!"—*Shaun Taylor, age 14, Midlothian, Virginia*

Comeback Kid: Brandi Chastain (of World Cup shirt-waving fame) kicked the ball into her own net during the U.S. team's match against Germany in the quarterfinal of the 1999 World Cup. She redeemed herself with a goal to tie the match 2–2. Her team went on to win it 3–2.

GAME DAY

The reason players join a soccer team to begin with is so they can play games. That's the fun part. Or it will be if you've practiced hard and your team is prepared.

According to University of Florida coach Becky Burleigh, game preparation is the most important key to success, since a well-prepared team is also a confident team. If players have gotten their offensive and defensive scenarios down in practice, on game day they'll be ready to go.

Games are like practice. Except they count.

GAME DAY TIP

When players arrive at the game field, they should warm up just as they do at practice with light jogging, dynamic warm-up exercises, calisthenics, and easy soccer moves. Likewise, after the game, they should take a few minutes to cool down and stretch.

So what strategy should a coach adopt for game day? Whatever approach best utilizes her players' talents and downplays their weaknesses. She will probably start out with players assigned to positions in a certain formation, and she may make slight adjustments at half-time, keeping in mind that during any match, unexpected scenarios come up and players must learn to adapt on the run. Literally.

But many scenarios are common and *can* be anticipated. The plays that follow are part of almost every match.

Rev it up for game day.

Short and sweet.

KICKOFFS

Play begins with a kickoff, and in soccer—unlike the other kind of football—the kicking team retains possession until it scores a goal, the ball goes out of bounds, or the other team takes it away.

The kicking team should strive to maintain possession of the ball. The best way for young players to accomplish this is to have the kicker roll the ball forward (or make a short pass) to a teammate, aiming to move the ball to the outside of the field and down toward the goal. Basically, the kickoff formation (for both offense and defense) is very similar to the playing formation.

FREE KICKS (DIRECT AND INDIRECT)

Direct

Since the kicker may shoot and score a goal without the ball touching another player, she should strive for a hard, straight shot, aiming for either side of the goal, away from the keeper. If possible, she should try not to look directly at the goalie (this could break her concentration) or her intended target (this could give away her intent). To defend against direct kicks, players need to learn to build a wall—that is, stand together side by side in a line, hoping to block the goal.

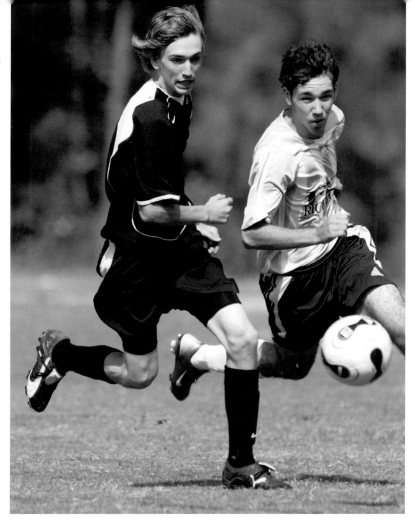

Mark your man.

Indirect

To score a goal from an indirect kick, the ball must first touch another player after the kicker strikes the ball from the designated spot. Players on the kicking team should strive to be in motion to capitalize on the pass from their teammate. To defend against indirect kicks, players will also need to build a wall, but some players should remain open to mark and defend against attackers.

PENALTY KICKS

Penalty kicks are taken from the penalty mark by a player from the team that was fouled. Since no players besides the keeper are allowed to defend the kick, it's a great idea to choose a very strong, accurate shooter to take the kick. Both offense and defense should practice moving into the penalty area and quickly reacting to a ball in play (if a goal is not scored).

CORNER KICKS

The object of a corner kick is to get the ball into the goal area. Players can practice this by kicking to a teammate, who then kicks the ball toward the goal. A more advanced kicker may shoot for the goal himself, striving to put a spin on the ball so it moves in the direction of the goal.

If a defender intercepts the ball, she should clear it immediately out of harm's way with a long pass. Don't dribble near your own goal!

The goal of every match: good game.

DEFENSE

Tips for playing "D":

- Any player who loses the ball should recover and immediately go after it again. This makes sense not only because he is closest to the ball, but so that his team will have time to regroup into defensive mode.

- Strive for balance. Players nearest the ball play tight, staying close to their man or the man with the ball. Players far away play loose, spreading out a bit and anticipating the attackers' next move.

- Strive to gain possession. Once your team gets the ball, pass it or dribble it toward open space.

- Work together. The most effective way to play defense is with a little help. Double-teaming and pressuring attacking players works better than attempting to tackle them on your own.

- Practice marking or covering your man. Stand sideways to the direction of the pass so you can easily change directions and ideally, intercept the ball.

COMING TO TERMS

Advantage: A situation in which a team has possession of the ball and outnumbers the opposition near the opposing goal.

Assist: The pass(es) immediately preceding a goal. Note: Up to two assists may be credited for one goal.

At speed: Full speed.

Attacker: Any player on the team with possession of the ball.

Back: A defender.

Break: When a team moves the ball down the field quickly, hoping to close in on the opponent's goal before the defenders are able to catch up to them. (May create an advantage.)

Breakaway: When an attacker with the ball approaches the goal undefended and meets the goalkeeper in a one-on-one showdown.

Center: A pass from a player located near the sideline toward the middle of the field, used to move the ball closer to the goal. (Also called a "cross.")

Center circle: A circular marking with a 10-yard (9.1 m) radius in the center of the field where kickoffs are taken to start or restart the game.

Center spot: A small circular mark inside the center circle that denotes the center of the field.

Clear: To kick the ball away from one's goal.

Corner arc (or corner area): A quarter-circle with a 1-yard (0.9-m) radius located at each of the four corners of the field. Corner kicks must be taken from inside this arc.

Corner flag: The flag located at each of the four corners of the field, inside the corner area.

Crossbar: The 24-foot-long (7.3-m) beam that sits on top of the two goal posts.

Defenders: The players on the team without possession of the ball.

Defensive pressure: When one or more defenders closely mark a ball carrier to try to force him to lose the ball.

Draw: A game that ends in a tied score.

Far post: The goalpost farthest away from the ball.

Field: The rectangular area where soccer matches are played.

Formation: The arrangement of players on the field. Example: A 4-3-3 formation describes four defenders, three midfielders, and three forwards on the field.

Forward line: The three or four forwards (two wings or one or two strikers) who work together to try to score.

Goal: A score counting for one point, made when the ball completely crosses over the goal line and under the goalposts.

Goal area: The rectangular area 20 yards wide by 6 yards deep (18.3 m by 5.5 m) in front of each goal from which all goal kicks are taken.

Goal line (or end line): The line that runs the width of the field from sideline to sideline at the end of both sides of the field with the goal in the middle.

Goal mouth: The front opening of each goal.

Goalposts: The two posts, 8 feet high (2.4 m) and 24 feet (7.3 m) apart, that form the sides of a goal and support the crossbar.

Halftime: The break (usually from five to fifteen minutes) between the two periods of a game.

Halves (or periods): The segments of time into which a game is divided. Adult regulation games consist of two forty-five-minute halves.

Hat trick: Three or more goals scored in a game by a single player.

Kickoff: A free kick that starts the game, half, or overtime or that restarts play after a goal.

Man-to-man: A type of defense in which each defender is assigned to mark a different forward on the other team; the most common type of defense for national-level teams.

Match: A soccer game.

Midfield line or center line: The line that divides the field in half along its width.

Near post: The goalpost closest to the ball.

Net: Hemp, jute, or nylon cord draped over the frame of the goal and extending behind it. Sometimes refers to the goal itself.

On defense: Describes a team that does not have possession of the ball.

On offense: Describes a team in possession of the ball.

Overlap: When a defender runs forward on the left or right flank to become part of the attack.

Overtime: The extra periods played after a regulation game ends with a tied score; used in collegiate and championship international matches to determine a winner.

Pitch: A British term for the soccer field.

Points: A team statistic indicating its degree of success, calculated as follows: 2 points for a win (3 in the 1994 World Cup), 1 point for a tie, 0 points for a loss; also, an individual statistic for a player, calculated by totaling 2 points for each goal and 1 point for each assist.

Possession: Control of the ball.

Post: Goalpost or the area near it.

Receiver: A player who gets a pass from a teammate.

Regulation game: Two completed periods of a game, prior to any overtime or tiebreaker.

Save: When a goalkeeper blocks or stops a shot that would have gone into the goal without his intervention.

Shot: A ball kicked or headed by a player toward the opponent's net in an attempt to score a goal.

Sideline (or touchline): The line that runs along the length of the field on each side.

Stopper: The defender who marks the best scorer on the attacking team, often the opposition's striker.

Substitution: Replacement of one player on the field with another player not on the field; FIFA rules allow only three substitutions per game.

Sudden death: A type of overtime in which the first goal scored by a team ends the game and gives that team the victory.

Territory: The half of the field that a team defends.

Throw-in: A type of restart where a player throws the ball from behind his head with two hands while standing with both feet on the ground behind a sideline. A throw-in is taken by a player opposite the team that last touched the ball before it went out of bounds across a sideline.

Tiebreaker: A way to choose the winner of a match when teams are tied after overtime; in FIFA tournament play, a series of penalty kicks is taken by players from both teams, and the team that scores on more of its kicks is declared the winner.

Turnover: Loss of possession of the ball.

Zone defense: Type of defense where defenders cover a designated area instead of marking one player.

5: Training for Soccer

Workouts and Tips for Getting Game-Ready

Most soccer players stay in shape by playing soccer. Athletes who play year-round have an edge. According to U.S. Men's National Team fitness coach Pierre Barrieu, the ideal scenario for serious soccer players is training every day or at least five days a week.

For players who take an off-season, staying in shape takes some dedication. Some athletes do it simply by running several days a week and taking a ball out and kicking it around as often as possible. Others sign up to play other sports such as lacrosse, hockey, or basketball. Some athletes follow preseason training programs designed by their coaches. (For a sample program, please see Appendix A.)

But whether you're a Manchester United veteran or a sophomore hoping to make the high school varsity team, you should arrive at your first practice fit and ready to go.

RUN, RUN, RUN!

Sure, soccer players need the moves. But they also need endurance to keep moving—to maintain the pace of a non-stop game with only a short break at halftime. There's only one way to increase endurance: by running. And running a lot. Players should run as much as possible during practice and also on their own time.

"A player should be able to run between sixty to ninety minutes at a pretty high pace, depending on their age group," says coach Barrieu. "Once you achieve this, you can worry about the rest, which includes trying to become faster."

Soccer players run . . . a lot.

What's Cardio?

Soccer players run constantly—both in short bursts and for long stretches down the length of the field. For this reason, athletes must be in good cardiovascular shape. "Cardio" means heart, so when you "do cardio" you are improving your heart's ability to function and pump fresh blood to your muscles as you run. You are also strengthening your respiratory system, which is why you don't get out of breath as easily when you're in shape.

Endurance athletes such as soccer players should aim to train in their aerobic zone, the stage of a workout where the body utilizes stored oxygen, at 70 to 80 percent of the maximum heart rate. To calculate your estimated maximum heart rate, subtract your age from 220. Then calculate 70 to 80 percent of that number to get your zone.

For a 16-year-old:

Max heart rate: 220 – 16 = 204
80 percent of 204 = 163
70 percent of 204 = 142

So a 16-year-old should aim for a heart rate between 142 and 163 beats per minute during her workout. Measure your heart rate by putting your index finger on the large artery of your wrist or the neck and counting the pulse beats for ten seconds. Then, multiply this number by six. Even better, use a heart-rate monitor!

If you don't have a stopwatch or clock to calculate an accurate heart rate, a good indicator that you are training in your desired aerobic zone is when you can't easily carry on a conversation but you are not yet out of breath.

Sweating can cause soccer players to lose up to seven pounds of body weight in one match.

Run! Faster!

Since soccer players constantly change their pace, running long distances followed by short sprints, often with a change of direction, they should train in similar fashion. In other words, you'll benefit more from training sessions that mimic a game than from just jogging or running for a half an hour straight.

One well-known training method is Fartlek (Swedish for "speed play") conditioning, where athletes are literally put through their paces for a predetermined time. During Fartlek sessions, athletes work continuously but vary the intensity level to challenge the muscles and increase endurance. Sample Fartlek session:

- Warm-up with a steady jog (10 minutes)
- Run hard at 75 percent of fastest-possible pace (90 seconds)
- Jog (45 seconds)
- Sprint (10 seconds)
- Run backwards (30 seconds)
- Walk (30 seconds)
- Run hard (60 seconds)
- Repeat entire session three to four times.

Note: Athletes should work at 60 to 80 percent of their maximum heart rate. Total session should last forty-five minutes or longer.

STRENGTH TRAINING

Traditionally, soccer players have been lean, mean, and fast, not big and bulky. So it's no surprise that until recently, many professional teams and competitive college and high school programs did not include weight lifting as part of their training regimen.

As a young player, L.A. Galaxy star Landon Donovan did not lift weights. "I always thought weights were more for football and baseball players." But while working out with the U.S. Men's National Team, he became a believer. "We're not in there trying to bench three hundred pounds," he says. "That's not relevant to soccer. We focus more on the core, hips, and shoulders because that's where we need strength to hold someone off or get to a ball."

Although the topic is still controversial, especially regarding young players, the trend is definitely shifting toward incorporating some weight training along with other strength and conditioning exercises into soccer players' routines. According to U.S. Men's National Team fitness coach Pierre Barrieu, "It's never too young to be aware that there are things you can do besides just playing. You can start as young as 10 when it comes to doing calisthenics or using your own body weight to train. But only players who have already gone through puberty should start a regular weight training program."

As long as players do their exercises with proper form, weight training can provide many benefits, including:

- Increased strength
- Increased confidence
- Increased speed
- Increased flexibility and range of motion
- Increased explosiveness
- Injury prevention

WHAT TO WORK, AND WHEN

Soccer players, who often develop very muscular legs just by playing the game, are well advised not to neglect their upper bodies during training. "We don't use the upper body that much, so we have to work the upper body during training to compensate," says Barrieu.

But despite all the running soccer players do, they need to work the legs in a more focused way during training as well. "The demands of the game put a lot of stress on the legs, so they are going to get stronger," Barrieu explains. "But while the quads get stronger, the hamstrings are getting weaker so you have to work them."

In general, to develop maximum strength an athlete should plan on four days of weight training a week (two days focusing on the upper body and two days working the lower body). These workouts are often combined with cardio by lifting weights first, then going for a run or a swim. Many athletes today also practice circuit training, a highly time-efficient gym workout in which they combine an aerobic workout and weight work at the same time by moving quickly from machine to machine without resting. Circuit training is usually done when endurance (very important in soccer) is being emphasized over strength.

The off-season is when many soccer players focus on increasing their strength through weight training. But since so many soccer players now compete year-round, it's a good idea to consult with your coach and trainer about what your specific routine should be.

There are many excellent resources to consult about exercising with weights. Many players and coaches consult the Web sites http://www.sport-fitness-advisor.com/soccertraining.html and http://www.soccerfitness.net. Other good sources include *Supertraining* by Mel Siff and *The Strength and Conditioning Journal*, a magazine published by the National Strength and Conditioning Association.

College and pro soccer players have been known to run up to nine miles during a match.

THE BASICS

Here are a few basic weight-training exercises you can do using just a few free weights and a bench. Remember, as a rule, soccer players work with lighter weights, performing a higher number of reps to increase endurance. But to increase strength (during the off season), you'll want to lift slightly heavier weights for fewer reps. Off season: Try to pick a weight you can lift slowly up to eight or nine times. On season: Try to pick a weight you can lift slowly ten to twelve times.

Bench Press (works the chest) Lie on your back on a bench. Your feet should be flat on the floor. Grasp one dumbbell in each hand, bend your arms, and hold the dumbbells at shoulder level, as close to the shoulders as possible Slowly lower the weights to just above your chest, then raise them straight up, extending your arms fully.

Do three sets, 8 to10 reps each.

Military Press (works the shoulders) Sit on the end of the bench or stand up straight. Pick up the weights and bring them to shoulder level with your elbows down at your sides. Lift the weights directly over your head, hold, then lower and return to starting position.

Do three sets, 8 to 10 reps each.

Biceps Curl (works the biceps) Sit on the end of the bench or stand up straight. Hold the weights with an underhand grip, resting them gently on the tops of your thighs. Bend your elbows and lift the weights slowly up to your chest. Then slowly lower them, keeping arms in line with your shoulders.

Do three sets, 8 to10 reps each.

STAND AND DELIVER

Often the best "weights" to use during training, especially for young players or those new to strength training, is your own body weight. The key is to use proper form and do the exercise slowly. The following moves can be performed on the floor or a mat. Athletes can also do these exercises outside on the field. Some exercises require a medicine ball or its larger, lighter cousin, the stability ball. (Both medicine balls and stability balls are effective pieces of equipment because they are more pliable and less stable than the hard ground. The body has to work against a ball, pushing it down to keep it stable, which increases the benefit of the exercise.)

Deep-Knee Squat

- Stand with your feet hip distance apart and knees loose, not locked. (See "It's Universal" on page 118 for a further description of the ideal stance).
- Extend your arms directly out in front of you for balance.
- Keeping your knees behind your toes, slowly lower into a squatting position until your thighs are parallel to the floor.
- Slowly return to a standing position.
- Do three sets, 8 to 10 reps each.

The U.S. National Team lifts weights two to three times a week during its training camp.

Lateral Jumps

- Stand on your left leg.
- Jump sideways to your right (approximately 6 to 8 inches) and land on your right leg on the mat.
- Keep your right knee soft to absorb the force and use your ankle, knee, and core to stabilize.
- Jump back to your left leg and repeat.
- Do three sets of 8 to 10 reps each.

Single-Leg Medicine Ball Reach

- Stand on your slightly bent right leg.
- Hold a medicine ball in front of your chest.

- Without dropping your chest toward the floor, rotate your torso 90 degrees to the right. Keep your head level and eyes on the ball.
- Return to start position.
- Do one set of 8 to 10 reps on each side.

Players with access to a gym, or even a few hand weights or dumbbells at home, can add the following strength training exercise several times a week.

Dumbbell Push Press

- Begin standing with your knees slightly flexed.
- Hold dumbbells at shoulder level.
- Drive dumbbells straight overhead by extending your hips, knees, and ankles simultaneously.
- Finish with your arms straight overhead and knees slightly bent.
- Do three sets of 8 to 10 reps.

It's Universal

Trainers around the world are well acquainted with a stance known as the "universal sports position."

Top-level athletes in every sport, from golf to surfing to football, strike a pose at a key point in their movement where they are semi-crouched on the balls of their feet, with hands in front and torso centered over the lower body. They are balanced, prepared to move in any direction—front, back, left, right.

This position, also known as "the athletic stance," is perfect for soccer players, who perform many explosive movements (cutting, dodging, faking) during a game. So, if you want to boost acceleration, agility, and your vertical leap, start by getting your torso in line.

To begin, a player stands with his feet hip distance apart, toes and heels in line, knees slightly bent, and arms down at his sides. Next he brings his arms out in front of him—elbows are bent, palms are flexed slightly.

Bring it on. This guy is ready.

Core Support

A strong and stable core, also known as the midsection of the body where the abdominals, obliques, and back extensors help brace the spine, is incredibly important to soccer players, who need to be able to move in every direction. All movements—every kick, dodge, fake, sprint—start from this area.

"Everything is predicated on how strong your core is," says the L.A. Galaxy's Landon Donovan. "The stronger it is, the more explosive you are. It enables you to cut that much quicker and get to the ball a half-second sooner. That could mean a goal—or even the World Cup. It sounds like a cliché, but trust me, that kind of stuff happens, and it's this training that makes the difference."

Trainer Pierre Barrieu always makes core training a priority, with the focus on stability. "What links the upper body to the lower body is the core," he says. "When the upper body is going right, the lower is going left. Everything connects from the hips."

The following exercises are best done inside on a mat. You'll need a stability ball or medicine ball for most of the moves.

Bird Dog

- Begin on all fours, with your knees directly under your hips, your hands directly under your shoulders, and your feet parallel.
- Without arching your back, straighten your right arm and left leg so they form a straight line with the body. Keep your head down.
- Hold the position for eight counts, then lower your arm and leg.
- Do three sets of 8 to10 reps on each side.

Forward Roll

- Kneel with your forearms resting on a stability ball.
- Raise your hips so that your body is in plank position, with only your feet touching the ground.
- Maintaining a straight line from shoulders to feet, use your forearms to roll the ball forward until it's past your shoulders.
- Roll the ball back and return to the starting position.
- Do three sets of 8 to 10 reps each.

Supine Bounce

- Lie on your back with your legs straight and the stability ball between your feet.
- Without allowing your back to arch, raise your legs so that the ball is 2 inches above the floor.
- Release the ball so it bounces off the floor, then catch it between your feet.
- Do three sets of 8 to10 reps each.

Pepper Catch

- Sit on the floor with your knees bent and your feet just slightly off the floor.
- Have a partner toss a medicine ball to you.
- Catch the ball, then stabilize and throw the ball back without twisting your hips.
- Do three sets of 8 to10 reps each.

> "You may have the best feet in the world but if you're not in the right spot at the right time, it doesn't matter."
>
> —PIERRE BARRIEU, U.S. MEN'S NATIONAL TEAM FITNESS COACH

Back Extension

- Lie on your stomach on a stability ball with your chest hanging over the edge of the ball.
- Place your hands behind your head, elbows out to the sides, and lift your chest off the ball.
- Hold, then return to the starting position.
- Do three sets of 8 to 10 reps each.

Hip Raise

- Lie on your back on the floor with your feet on a stability ball, knees bent at a 90-degree angle.
- Raise your hips so that only your shoulder blades touch the floor.
- Form a straight line from shoulders to knees; hold.
- Lower your body back to the floor.
- Do three sets of 8 to 10 reps each.

NOTES ON STRETCHING

According to the American College of Sports Medicine, stretching, if done regularly and carefully, can increase range of motion in the joints, nourish muscle tissue, improve coordination and posture, and contribute to improved athletic performance. That said, the current school of thought discourages stretching cold muscles. In other words, you should never start a workout by stretching. Stretch only *after* a warmup or, even better, after a full workout.

Not convinced? Trainer Pierre Barrieu says static stretching before a performance will actually make you slower. So, save it for later.

Although for years coaches and athletes believed stretching could prevent injury, there have been no conclusive studies published to prove this. However, most trainers find that stretching can help an athlete recover from an injury. In any case, stretching improves flexibility, which is always a plus.

For a more detailed explanation of stretching, including diagrams of sample stretches, two good sources are the *Personal Trainer's Manual,* from the American Council on Exercise, and *Stretching* by Bob Anderson (Shelter Publications).

STRETCHING TIPS

- Stretch only when your body is warmed up.
- Never bounce while stretching.
- Stretch until muscles feel tight but stop before you feel pain.
- Hold stretches for ten to thirty seconds.
- Don't hold your breath while stretching. Take deep, full breaths.
- Stretch as often as possible—every day if you can.

Stretch only when you're warm.

What qualities should coaches look for in a young player? "Game intelligence, technique, and speed. But if the technique and attitude is there, then you can build on that."—FORMER ARSENAL COACH ARSÈNE WENGER

FEED ME

Food is fuel for athletes. A midfielder who doesn't consume enough calories soon finds herself running out of steam, whether she's in the gym or out on the playing field.

Quantity is important. But what and when a player eats is just as important as how much she eats. Despite the current low-carb trend, it's important for athletes to remember that they rely on carbohydrates for performance, especially wholesome, complex carbohydrates, such as those found in multigrain bread or oatmeal. Athletes need to maximize glycogen (carbohydrate) stores during training as well as when it really counts—during competition.

Protein is an important part of the diet, but athletes may find that too much protein hinders their performance, since the body digests proteins relatively slowly. Therefore, it's especially important to avoid too much protein right before a game.

Every player should make it a point to formulate her own diet plan and experiment to find out what approach works best. (Just don't experiment on game day!) Coaches are a great resource for nutrition tips, and there are many excellent books on the topic of nutrition for athletes who play endurance sports such as soccer. (Check out *The Sports Nutrition Guidebook*, Third Edition, 2008, by Nancy Clark.)

In addition to eating a well-balanced diet, the best thing a player can do to enhance his performance and keep from feeling fatigued is to

Drink water before, during, and after a game.

drink water. Hydration is extremely important, especially on game day. An athlete should remember to drink water the day before a game or a practice and throughout the day leading up to the game. If he waits to hydrate while playing, it may be too late.

According to the National Athletic Trainers' Association (NATA), a player should drink at least 16 to 20 ounces (0.5 to 0.6 l) of fluids approximately two hours before working out. Many coaches tell their players to drink up to 100 ounces of water or water mixed with sports drinks in the course of a day, especially during the hottest months of the year.

Note: Although water should be your main drink, sports drinks are fine to put in the mix, especially after a game or practice when you need to replace electrolytes.

Here are some sample menu items, courtesy of the *Parent/Player Handbook* compiled by FC Richmond (Richmond, Virginia).

Pre-Match Meals

The main goal of a pre-game meal is to elevate glycogen levels by eating foods rich in carbohydrates. Be sure not to eat so much food that you feel uncomfortable and won't be able to play well.

High Carbohydrate Dinner or Lunch
(three to four hours prior to game)

- Chicken breast, mashed potatoes, vegetables
- Rice (steamed or boiled)
- Soup (avoid heavy or creamed soup, also chili)
- Baked potato (light butter, low-fat or no-fat sour cream)
- Deli sandwich (lean meats, veggies, light mayo, little cheese)
- Thick-crust cheese or vegetable pizza
- Peanut butter sandwich
- Grilled or roasted chicken sandwich
- Pasta salad with low-fat dressing
- Salads
- Pasta and marinara sauce with bread

High Carbohydrate Breakfast (three hours prior to game)

- Fruit
- Waffles
- Pancakes (light butter and syrup)
- Cold or hot cereal
- Low-fat yogurt
- Toast, bagel, English muffin, bran muffin
- Pasta or pasta salad

- Fresh fruit (apples, bananas, grapes, oranges)
- No greasy foods or heavy meats (hash browns, breakfast steaks, ham, or sausage)

Light Snacks (one to two hours prior to game in moderate quantity)

- Bagel or English muffin
- Raisins, dried fruit
- Yogurt with cereal or fruit
- Pretzels, unsalted peanuts
- Whole-wheat toast or bread
- Crackers
- Fresh fruit (apples, bananas, grapes, oranges)
- Popcorn (no salt/butter)
- Granola or energy bar
- Cold or hot cereal

Note: After the game, players should consume carbohydrate-rich fluids and foods as soon as possible (at least within one to two hours after hard exercise) to replace the glycogen they burned during the game.

WHY SOCCER?

"I started playing soccer at age 5. I had a lot of energy so that was one way I could use up some of my energy and have fun. I played on a co-ed team, and I was not afraid of the boys. I could run just as fast and be just as tough as them. I loved watching my brother play. He was a couple of years older, so I went to all his games. One time a coach told his team that if someone could stop number 11, which was my brother, he would cut his ponytail off. They never did stop him."—*Katie Leech, Age 15, Westminster, Maryland*

NUTRITION TIPS

- Each meal should consist of a lean protein (chicken, tuna, tofu), fibrous carbohydrate (lettuce, cauliflower, cucumber), and healthy fat (olive oil, nuts, fish).

- Avoid high-fat and high-sugar snacks and meals. These can slow you down faster than a tough defender.

- Try to get your vitamins from real food as opposed to supplements. Energy from protein, minerals, and fiber is best utilized by the body when it comes from actual calories.

- On workout days, be sure to consume plenty of water—at least half your body weight in ounces (so a 150-pound player should drink 75 ounces).

- Carbo-load throughout the week before a game and for the first four hours afterward for optimum recovery.

- Don't overeat late the night before a game. Also, try to eat a light breakfast the morning before a game or practice.

- Remember, during a workout or game you are burning what you ate and stored twenty-four to forty-eight hours earlier.

- Experiment with diet and hydration during practice—not on game day!

- Avoid the drive-thru and other places serving fast (i.e., high-fat) foods.

- Avoid food and drinks containing caffeine since they cause dehydration.

- Aim for 60 percent of calories from carbs, 15 percent from protein, and 25 percent from fat.

Active rest: An easy activity designed to keep a player warm.

Aerobic: A stage of a workout when all of the body's need for oxygen is met by what is being inhaled and what is already stored in the body. This state can continue for a long time.

Anaerobic: A stage of a workout when the body's need for oxygen is not met by what is being inhaled and what is already stored in the body. This state cannot continue for long because it causes a pairful buildup of lactic acid in the muscles.

During college, Kyle Rote, Jr., played football and soccer and ran track. Originally, he began playing soccer to stay in shape during the off-season, but then he fell in love with the game and made it his number one focus. The result? He became an enormous star pro soccer player in the 1970s.

6: PRACTICE, PRACTICE, PRACTICE

How to Get Fast, Get Focused, and Get Good Feet

No doubt about it. Pelé and Beckham and Mia were born to play soccer. They all had a natural gift. But it was practice, practice, and more practice that made them truly great. Young players who aspire to greatness—or who simply aspire to have a great time playing soccer—can get there if they're willing to practice too.

FOOT FINESSE

According to Arsenal coach Arsène Wenger, the focus of every youth development program should be teaching soccer's essential skills. "The most important thing for players under 14 years old is technique," Wenger says. "After age 14, speed becomes more and more important. Not physical speed but reaction and speed with the ball."

Begin with the basics.

That said, many coaches agree that players should be given the opportunity to learn skills at their own pace. "Young players need freedom of expression to develop as creative players," Wenger says. "They should be encouraged to try skills without fear of failure. At a young age, winning is not the most important thing. The important thing is to develop creative and skilled players with good confidence."

And players should start with the aspects of technique they can actually use. National Soccer Hall of Fame president Steve Baumann, who spent many years as a high-school and college coach, explains, "You don't need to go through all the skills with really young players because mostly, the ball will be on the ground. So, teaching them a chest trap when they're six years old doesn't make a lot of sense. If you've ever watched seven-year-olds play, there isn't a lot of heading going on!"

So it's agreed. Young players need to start with basic, individual skills. When it comes to soccer, the basics begin with dribbling.

DRIBBLING

Dribbling is the skill soccer players use to move the ball down the field using only their feet. When a

Dribbling—from the inside out.

player is dribbling the ball, she is actually pushing the ball by tapping or kicking it with any part of her foot. As a player improves, she will be able to not only advance the ball down the field, but elude defenders at the same time. Experienced players eventually progress to speed dribbling, where they kick the ball out several feet in front of them and sprint to catch up to it. But this is a very advanced move.

As early as possible, coaches should teach players to dribble with both their right and left feet. Every player has a dominant foot, but striving to dribble with both will help when it comes time to stop, slow down, or change direction on the field. Coaches should also teach players to dribble with all parts of the foot. It's best to begin at a slow pace: New players should try dribbling at a walk before they try jogging or running. Next, coaches can try varying the pace, having players dribble fast down the field, then dribble more slowly around cones to get used to changing directions. When players have mastered the basics, it's time to try more advanced drills where defenders try to take the ball away.

DRIBBLING DOS AND DON'TS

Great dribblers make great soccer players. For the most control:

- Use the inside of the foot to push the ball.

- Use the outside of the foot when running fast.

- Use the sole of the foot to stop the ball or pull it back to change direction.

- Avoid using the toe, which may unintentionally cause you to kick the ball away from you. It's much easier to control the ball with the inside and outside of the feet.

Use the instep to great effect.

DRIBBLING TIPS

- Keep the ball near the body and close to the feet.
- Ai-m for a soft touch. If you kick too hard, the ball will get away from you.
- Take it slow. If you run too fast, you may lose control of the ball.
- Learn to dribble with each foot.
- Learn to dribble with all parts of each foot.
- Use your instep (the arched middle portion of the top of the foot, between the ankle and the toes) to make sharp cuts with the ball.
- Don't stare at the ball. Look up so you can see what's going on around you.
- Shield the ball from defenders by keeping your body between your opponent and the ball.
- Keep your knees bent and your body balanced so you can change direction easily.

It's all about balance.

"David and our three sons put me in goal and kick footballs at me. I'm the goalie of the family."

—VICTORIA "POSH SPICE" BECKHAM

SHIELDING, FAKES, AND OTHER FANCY FOOTWORK

Once a player masters basic dribbling, he moves on to fancier moves. The first thing he'll want to learn is how to change direction and turn the ball. Players need these skills to clear defenders, move down the field, and get in a position to score.

The two most fundamental change-of-direction moves are the cut and the step over. Players should learn to do each move with both the right and the left foot.

The Cut

- While moving down the field with the ball, tap it forward and run toward it.
- Stop the ball with the outside or inside of the foot, and turn it away from the defender.
- Pivot away from the defender, and run with the ball in a different direction or look for a teammate open for a pass.

The Step-Over

- At half speed, move toward the defender and lean away from the direction you intend to move the ball (or pull your leg back to fake an intended kick).
- Step over the ball.
- Plant the foot you've just stepped with, and then immediately pivot away from the defender.
- Tap the ball away from the defender with the step-over foot and then take off!

Turning the Ball

When changing directions, make sure you have enough space to turn the ball.

How to Do It

- Turn away from the defender; then use the inside or the outside of the foot to change the direction the ball is moving, depending on where the opponent is positioned.
- Avoid exposing the ball to the defender or turning toward him.
- After you turn the ball and/or switch the ball to dribble with the opposite foot, speed up your pace and dribble away.

"Run hard in practice so you can run past people in games."

—U.S. MEN'S NATIONAL FITNESS COACH PIERRE BARRIEU

Shielding

To protect the ball from a defender, a player frequently needs to shield the ball.

How to Do It

- Stand sideways next to the defender, positioning your body between him and the ball.
- Extend your arm toward the defender for balance and to give yourself space.
- Keep the ball and your foot away from the opponent, and keep your head up to look for open teammates.

When attempting to beat a defender, sell the fake. Look at your opposite hand (away from the direction you intend to go) to throw the defender off.

Passing

Passing is the way that soccer players connect the dots. By passing effectively to one another, teammates can maintain control of the ball and put themselves in position to score. Great passing teams win soccer matches.

What makes a good pass?

- **Accuracy:** The best passes land right at your teammate's feet.
- **Intensity:** Not too hard, not too soft.
- **Timing:** The ball should reach your teammate so he doesn't have to stop or scramble to receive the ball.
- **Deception:** Don't let your opponent know where you intend your pass to go.
- **Angle:** The correct approach will get the ball to its intended destination.

Although occasionally a player makes a square (sideways) pass or a back (backwards) pass, most passes move forward.

Eventually, passing means scoring.

Short Passes

Also known as "push passes," short passes are the most common because they tend to be the most accurate. As the name implies, short passes are short (usually 20 yards [18.3 m] or less, and shorter for very young players). Accuracy is definitely more important than power.

How to Do It

- Place the non-kicking foot several inches to the side of the ball, and bend the knee slightly.
- Turn the kicking foot perpendicular to the intended path of your pass, with the toes higher than the heel.
- Keep your ankle locked.
- Make contact with the center of the ball with the inside of your foot as you swing the kicking leg forward from the hip and knee.
- Lean back slightly, and follow through with your leg in the direction you want the ball to go.

Long Passes

Also known as "drives," long passes require more strength and power than short passes, but players should remember that, as with all passes, accuracy is important. What good is a ball sent sailing down the field into the path of a waiting defender?

Different types of long passes are used in different situations such as goal kicks, corner kicks, long-distance shots, and free kicks. Lofted passes (those that travel high in the air rather than low to the ground) are usually safer since they are more difficult for opponents to intercept.

How to Do It

- Approach the ball at a slight angle, and shorten your steps as you get closer to the ball.
- Point the support foot toward the target (where you want the ball to go), and plant it a few inches behind the ball.
- Lean back slightly, and swing your leg backward from the knee and hip.
- Keep your ankle locked with the toes of the kicking foot held slightly lower than the heel.
- Strike the ball with the instep of your foot.
- Follow through past the original position of the ball.

Note: The lower you strike the ball, the higher it will go. For a kick of medium height,

strike the ball several inches below the center. For maximum height, strike the ball just above the turf with your toe just under the ball. For greater distance, try to lengthen your approach to the ball and swing your leg farther back before you kick. The best chip shots lob the ball with plenty of backspin to keep the pass from traveling too far.

Chipping

When players are under pressure, one type of pass (generally a short one) that is very useful is the chip. Players use this move to lob the ball over a defender's head and pass it to a teammate. Because it's a great way to literally skip over defenders, players also frequently chip the ball when shooting on goal.

How to Do It

- Approach the ball from a slight angle.
- Plant your support foot next to and slightly behind the ball.
- Swing your kicking foot back behind your body from the hip and knee, with your ankle locked.
- With your heel close to the ground, drive your toe under the ball and strike the ball with your instep.

  Don't follow through the way you would on other passes; you're striving for arc, not distance.

PASSING TIP

Every player should strive to make crisp, controlled passes. If she strikes the ball too softly or kicks it too slowly, it will be easy for a defender to intercept. If she kicks it too hard or too fast, the ball may get away.

Advanced Passing

As players progress, they will want to learn more complicated passes such as first-touch passes, where a player makes the pass with his first touch of the ball (in other words, a pass from a pass). This skill comes in handy when the pressure is on. But for the most part, U-10 and younger players should stop the ball after receiving a pass before they move it downfield. Especially for beginning players, simple, straightforward kicks and passes are best.

SWEET!

Every soccer player has a "sweet spot" on his foot, a point of contact somewhere on the laces of the shoe that will give him a perfect, uniform kick every time. To find yours, sit on the ground with your feet extended in front of you. Hold a ball above your head and drop it toward the laces of your shoe and raise your foot until it meets the ball. You'll find the sweet spot when the ball goes straight back up without any spin or rotation. Once you find it, be sure to practice shooting and passing the ball from this spot on your foot.

SHOOTING

Players can pass all day, but unless they shoot on goal, their team will never win the game. Both passing and shooting share many common characteristics, but think of shooting as the big brother of passing. Shots on goal are passes that count.

Like passes, shots on goal should be accurate. But while passes are often short, shots usually travel a greater distance to reach their target. Also, shooters often kick the ball harder than passers because they are trying to get the ball past the goalie, not into a teammate's possession.

Instep Power Drive

There are many different ways to shoot the ball in different game situations. One of the most common is the Instep Power Drive, which utilizes the power and accuracy of the top middle part of the foot.

How to Do It

- With the head steady and the hips squared toward the target, approach the ball from behind and at a slight angle.
- Plant your non-kicking foot beside the ball, about a foot away, and draw your kicking leg back behind your body.
- Keep your body and head over the ball, and swing the kicking leg forward from the hip and knee.
- With your instep perpendicular to the ground and your toe pointing down, strike the ball with the instep and follow through in the direction of the goal.

Shooting moves for more advanced players include the half, side, and full volleys, shots taken when balls are moving fast and defenders are in hot pursuit.

Half Volley

In this move, also sometimes called "shooting the ball on the short hop," a player strikes the ball in midair instead of taking the time to control it or stop it first.

Side Volley

A player approaches a high-bouncing ball from the side to take a shot or redirect a pass.

Full Volley

A player approaches a high-bouncing ball from the front to take a shot or redirect a pass.

Penalty Kick

Also known as a "spot kick," a penalty kick is the ultimate free kick awarded to a team when a member of the opposing team commits a serious foul in the penalty area. Any player on the team (not just the player who was fouled) may take the kick. Only the kicker and the goalkeeper are allowed in the penalty area during the kick. After the shot is taken, players should be ready to rush the goal in case the goalkeeper knocks the ball away but allows a rebound.

How to Do It

- Approach the ball from a slight angle from approximately 6 to 8 feet (1.8 to 2.4 m) away.
- Place your support foot several inches from the side of the ball, turned so that it is pointing slightly away from the target.
- Swing the kicking foot from your hip and knee, toe pointed down and ankle locked. (Note: If you are right-footed, lean slightly left. If you are left-footed, lean slightly right.)
- At the end of the kick, point the kicking foot outward and strike the ball with the inside arch of your foot.
- Follow through in the direction of your shot.

TIP FOR PLAYERS

As you get more experience, you will learn not to shoot directly at the goalie during penalty kicks and other shots on goal. The best spots to aim for are the corners of the goal.

BENDS, BICYCLES, AND BANANAS

Soccer gets really exciting as players develop enough confidence and skill to use magnificent moves such as the banana kick—a shot where the ball actually dips and curves—to deflect the ball away from defenders and oftentimes to score a goal.

When a soccer player "bends it," she is literally bending the path of the ball around the opposition by using the inside of the foot to curve the ball's trajectory. The kicker approaches the ball from an angle while concentrating her weight on the outside of the support leg as it remains on the ground next to the ball. She then leans backward and away from the ball, points her toes slightly up, and hits the outside of the ball with the inside of her foot.

It's like riding a bike.

In the dramatic bicycle kick (also called a "scissors kick")—a move seen mostly in the pros—the player falls backward parallel to the ground as a lofted ball approaches. He then "scissors" his legs, leading with one leg and following through with the other to snap at the ball. After the ball is on its way, the player braces himself with his arms for his inevitable fall. (Note: If you want to practice this move, try it first on the sand or on a mat, because you *will* fall!)

RECEIVING

One of the most important skills a soccer player learns is receiving a pass from a teammate. Basically, the move involves collecting the ball with any part of the body (except for the arms and hands), controlling it, and preparing to pass, dribble, or shoot. All in one move.

Most balls approach a player on the ground. These passes are received with either the right or left foot (the instep, sole, inside, or outside). Eventually, older players will also use their feet to receive bouncing balls or air balls.

Most passes are received on the inside of the foot.

Players should learn to receive on the outside of the foot as well.

Receiving a Rolling Ball

When a teammate is about to pass you the ball, face her so she knows you are ready.

How to Do It

- Once the ball is passed, immediately hustle toward it.
- Bend the knee of your supporting leg for balance.
- Raise the toes on the foot of your receiving leg, relax the foot, then meet the ball with the inside of the foot.
- Pull the leg back to slow the ball, push the ball to the side, and pivot.
- Dribble or pass the ball to a teammate.

Receiving an Air Ball

When an air ball is coming your way, check out other players' positions on the field to plan where you will play the ball after receiving it.

How to Do It

- Position your body to receive the ball directly in front of you.
- Rest your weight on your supporting leg, bending the knee slightly for balance.
- Raise your receiving foot several inches off the ground, in line with the approaching ball and parallel to the ground.
- When the ball makes contact with your foot, softly lower the foot and leg and guide the ball to the ground.

Note: Although players receive balls most often with the inside of the foot, they should also learn to receive with the outside of the foot and the instep. The steps for receiving with the outside of the foot are the same as those for receiving with the inside, except the area where the ball makes contact is smaller, so this move takes a little more practice. The steps for receiving with the instep are also the same, except players will need to accurately judge where the ball will land, which takes more finesse.

Receiving with the Thigh

Sometimes air balls or bouncing passes meet a player above ground level, making it necessary to receive with the thigh or knee. Players are smart to turn to receive the ball with the thigh, since ball-to-knee contact can be painful!

- Stand in front of the ball and flex the knee of your receiving leg.
- Raise the leg so it is parallel to the ground and positioned to receive the ball.
- Stop the ball, cushioning it by slightly dropping the knee as the ball lands at mid-thigh.
- Guide the ball to drop to the ground; then trap it with your foot.

Receiving with the Chest

Air balls or bouncing passes sometimes meet a player at chest level.

- Stand facing the ball, and align yourself in its path.
- Hold your arms out to the sides for balance, arch your back, and puff out your chest.
- Allow the ball to make contact to the right or left of the center of your chest. (Girls should make contact with the ball slightly higher.)
- When the ball touches your body, exhale and pull your chest back slightly to cushion the ball.
- Guide the ball to the ground, and trap it with your foot.

HEADING

In soccer, players often need to use their heads—literally—by "hitting" the ball with the forehead (right between the eyebrows and the hairline). Heading is usually a way to clear the ball far away from pursuing attackers, but players can also head the ball to pass to a teammate or even to score a goal.

How to Do It

- Stand in a balanced and relaxed position with feet shoulder width apart.
- Pull your head and body back; then, keeping the neck muscles tight, thrust your body forward to meet the ball, hitting it with your forehead.

When you have to, use your head.

TIP FOR PLAYERS

Beginners should use an underinflated ball or a soft foam ball when learning heading.

Try not to head the ball with the top of your head; it will probably bounce in an unintended direction, and, worse, it will probably hurt. When using your head to make a shot on goal, it's best to be relatively close to the goal. Otherwise, get control by heading, and then use a kick to make the shot.

THROW-INS

Although soccer is mostly a game of the feet, players need to be prepared for the throw-in, the method of restarting the game in which a player throws the ball back into play from the sideline. Most throw-ins, especially during games with younger players, are short. More advanced players should be ready for longer throw-ins, which require more power.

How to Do It

- Stand with both feet behind the sideline. Feet should be shoulder width apart, and knees should be loose.
- Spot your target (an open or soon-to-be-open teammate), but try not to look right at him.
- Place both hands on the ball, grasping it from the sides, step to the line, and lift the ball back behind your head.
- Face the target, and throw the ball in a continuous motion. Release both hands at the same time.

TIP FOR PLAYERS

To get a little more power, players will take several steps or even run toward the sideline before throwing. Both feet should be on the ground during the release. Also, try not to put any spin on the ball.

TACKLING

True, most soccer players have assigned positions. But when the opposing team has the ball, every player switches to defensive mode. A defender who's not near the ball should mark an open player to prevent her from receiving a pass. Defenders near the ball should pounce on any opportunity to take it away by tackling, that is, using the foot to take the ball away from the attacker.

The object of the tackle: the ball.

When to Tackle

- When the ball is between the attacker's feet.
- When the ball is way out in front of the attacker.
- After the attacker makes a bad first touch.

How to Tackle

- Position yourself approximately 3 feet (0.9 m) from the attacker, with your feet staggered.
- Swing your foot backward.
- Bring the foot forward, flexing it, and block the ball with the foot.
- Extend your arms out for balance, lean your trunk slightly forward, and contact the ball with your foot.

TIP FOR PLAYERS

When looking to tackle an opponent, patience pays. Sometimes a defender has to wait for his opportunity to take the ball away. If he strikes too soon, he may lose the opportunity or, worse, get called for a foul.

COERVER COACHING

Every successful soccer coach spends a great deal of time on individual skills. Wiel Coerver, a world-famous Dutch coach, developed a method for teaching ball mastery skills as well as other components necessary to player development, such as passing and receiving, one-on-one attacking and receiving, speed, finishing, and group play. (For detailed information on the Coerver coaching method, camps, etc., check out http://www.coerver.com.)

Here are some of the Coerver method's Fast Footwork moves that help young players develop good feet:

Side to Side: Tap ball back and forth with the inside of the feet.

Pull-a-Vee: Push the ball forward and pull it back with the sole of the foot while turning it; then take the ball with the inside of the same foot.

Outside Roll: Roll the ball across your body from inside to outside with the outside and sole of the foot, and stop the ball with the inside of the same foot.

360: Push the ball forward; stop it with the sole of one foot while stepping past it; turn and drag ball back with the sole of the other foot; continue turning all the way around; and take the ball with the inside of the first foot.

KEEPER!

The goalkeeper plays a unique role—and often the most crucial role—on the soccer field. Obviously, he guards the goal and does everything possible to keep the other team from scoring. And though people say it's not the goalie's fault when a ball gets past him—after all, the ball had to get past a whole team of defenders even to be in his vicinity—every keeper feels responsible when a ball hits his net.

Besides being the keeper of the goal, the goalie is also a leader who calls out directions and instructions to his teammates from his unique vantage point overlooking the field. The keeper is really a combination of coach, conductor, and cheerleader. He's the team anchor who calls out instructions, directions, and plenty of encouraging chatter.

Goalkeepers use different equipment than other players (pads, gloves). They wear a different color uniform. They play by different rules (keepers can use their hands). And they also require a different set of skills than their ten teammates. True, keepers need to master basic soccer techniques such as dribbling, receiving, and passing. But they also need to practice goalie-specific skills such as making saves and distributing the ball.

MAKING SAVES

Before a keeper can do his most important job—stopping the ball—he needs to get ready. The first thing he does when he steps in goal is to assume the "ready stance." Similar to the universal position in all sports (see Chapter 5), this is a loose, relaxed (although alert!) standing position with his feet shoulder width apart, his hands out in front of him (flexible and ready) or slightly out to the side, and his weight resting on the balls of his feet, heels raised, toes pointing out. His body is bent slightly forward, his head is up, and his eyes are on the ball.

Stopping Shots

A goalkeeper varies her shot-stopping technique according to the type of shot: a ball coming toward her at ground level, at waist height, at chest height, or in the air.

How to Stop a Shot on the Ground

- From the ready stance, shuffle sideways and get in position between the ball and the goal.
- With knees bent and feet a few inches apart, bend forward at the waist as the ball rolls toward you.
- Extend your arms down with palms facing forward, and let the ball roll up onto your wrists and forearms.
- Stand upright and clutch the ball to your chest.

   Note: If it feels right, the keeper may want to kneel as he collects the ball.

Keeper at the ready.

FOR KEEPS

Most soccer aficionados call the guy who stands in the goal and gets to use his hands a "goalkeeper," or "keeper" for short. Some people call him a "goalie." But if they call him a "goaltender," they're betraying themselves as soccer neophytes.

How to Stop a Waist-High Shot

- From the ready stance, bend forward at the waist as the ball approaches and extend your arms down, palms facing forward.
- Receive the ball on your wrists and forearms, pull it tight against your chest, and step backward slightly to cushion the impact.

How to Stop a Chest-High Shot

The diamond grip.

- Assume the ready stance.
- As the ball arrives, position your hands in the W-grip position or in the diamond-grip position by forming either a W or a diamond behind the ball with your thumbs and index fingers.
- With elbows slightly flexed, extend your arms toward the ball and catch it with your fingertips.
- Pull the ball securely to your chest.

How to Stop a Shot in the Air

- Assume the ready stance, but crouch a little lower.
- Determine the path of the ball, move toward it, bend your front leg, and jump!
- Lift your arms overhead, and catch the ball at the highest point possible.
- Bring the ball securely to your chest before landing.

Note: If the ball comes toward the keeper high above his head, he may have to tip it, or push the ball over the crossbar (before it reaches the net) with the fingertips of one hand.

Dramatic Dives

No matter which direction a ball is coming from or how high, it may be just out of a goalkeeper's reach. In this instance, the goalie may have to punch the ball away, parry the ball, make a sliding save, or even dive for the ball.

How to Dive

- With the foot closest to the ball, step in the direction you're going to dive and push off that foot.
- Extend your arms and hands toward the ball with your hands in a sideways W-grip.
- Receive the ball on your fingertips and palms.
- Place your lower hand behind the ball, pull your elbows into the front of your body, and ground the ball with your upper hand as you land on your side.

Note: Diving is for U-12 players and up. A coach should first teach the keeper how to land safely (on her side, not her stomach!); then teach the takeoff part of the skill.

How to Slide

- Approach the ball with your body low.
- Drop to your side, and slide toward the ball.
- Extend your hands toward the ball.

- Collect the ball, and pull it in tightly toward your chest.

    Note: Keepers should attempt to slide only if they know they can reach the ball before the shooter is able to kick it again.

How to Trap

Finally, goalkeepers need to learn how to trap or collapse on the ball. Many saves are made this way, often under intense pressure.

- Collapse onto the side of your body (to distribute the impact evenly).
- Bring the ball in, and bend your top leg into your body.
- Stay on your side (never your back—you won't be able to control the ball as well!), and look downfield for the best place to distribute the ball.

How to Punch

This save comes in handy when a keeper finds himself in a crowd.

- Leap at the ball as if to catch it.
- Punch the ball to the side, out of harm's way.

    Ideally, make two fists first to avoid hurting your hands!

How to Parry

When a keeper can't catch a ball, she sometimes chooses to parry it by knocking or deflecting it over the crossbar or around the post.

- Reach (or jump) toward the middle of the approaching ball.
- Extend your arm or arms in the direction you want the ball to go, and punch it with the heel of your hand or hands.

Note: Learning how to protect the goal from enemy shots is the keeper's priority. Another important function is assisting defenders under pressure. A keeper should be prepared to receive a pass from her own teammates and immediately pass to another teammate or clear the ball downfield. (A keeper may not use her hands when receiving a pass from her own teammate.) Defenders should only pass to the keeper when she is wide open and not under attack. The last thing a defender wants to do is help the attacking team score or, worse, kick the ball past her own keeper!

TIP FOR COACHES

Coaching the keeper can be a challenge, especially for coaches who never played the position themselves. As players progress and need to learn more challenging moves, coaches should invite older players or coaches from college teams to come demonstrate and guest-coach at practice. They should also encourage keepers to sign up for specialized clinics.

DISTRIBUTING THE BALL

Sending the ball back into play after making a save may seem like the less glamorous part of goalkeeping. But distributing, especially when the keeper gets the ball directly into a teammate's path, is a very important skill that often affects the outcome of the match.

Timing is crucial. Since according to the *Laws of the Game*, a keeper has only six seconds to return the ball after making a save, quickness counts. So does accuracy. Simply punting the ball without considering where it will land is a risky venture.

Depending on the play, there are three ways a keeper distributes the ball: bowling, throwing, and kicking.

KEEPING SECRETS

World Cup veteran and English Premier League goalkeeper Kasey Keller gives this advice to up-and-coming keepers:

"There are no secrets. It's all about a few basic things. It's different ways to get the same job done—not to let the ball into the net. You have to have quite a bit of a thick skin to be a goalkeeper. You have to be able to put everything else aside. When you've made an error, you might have a lot of the game left. If you've gone into a shell and have a nightmare of a game, all of a sudden your team is trailing, 3–0. You have to live with that and tell yourself that the next game you have to play better."

Bowling

As the name implies, this method, best for short distances, involves rolling the ball down the field as if the keeper were bowling. The keeper places the ball in one hand, steps toward the target with the opposite foot, and releases the ball so it rolls smoothly at ground level without bouncing.

Throwing

This method, best for longer distances, involves an overhand throw much like throwing a baseball. The keeper holds the ball in the palm of her hand, steps toward the target, and throws.

GOALIE-SPEAK

A keeper is often in the best position to see what's going on, whether her team is attacking the opposite goal, or whether the pressure is on her own side. So, the keeper needs to talk to her teammates throughout the match. If she is in a position to reach the ball first, she yells, "Keeper!"

Or if she is open to receive a pass from a teammate under pressure, she yells, "Back!" She warns her team when defenders are en route: "Man on! Man on right!" And she lets them know when things are going right: "Back to the middle! There you go! Awesome!"

TIP FOR PLAYERS

Follow-through is the most important step in distributing, especially when b\owling or throwing, where you use the fingers of the throwing hand to follow through.

Kicking

This method is less accurate than bowling or throwing, but it's the best approach for clearing the ball far and fast downfield. To distribute the ball this way, keepers mostly use a drop kick (hold the ball in front of you, let the ball drop to the ground, and kick with the instep) or a full-volley punt (hold the ball in front of you, release it, and kick it before it hits the ground).

PUTTING TOGETHER THE PERFECT PRACTICE

Every practice begins with a good ten-minute warm-up. Start slowly by jogging or doing some easy shuttles, where you shuffle sideways back and forth, keeping your body low to the ground. Easy calisthenics such as jumping jacks are also a good way to get warm. Follow with dynamic stretching, which means stretching while moving, not while holding still.

This is important preparation for what's to come, according to U.S. Men's National Team fitness coach Pierre Barrieu: "When you stretch before practice or a game, you have to apply the same speed of contraction as during the game." Save static stretching (stretches you hold for thirty seconds) for the end of practice.

You're getting warmer!

Some dynamic warm-up stretches include:

- Hamstring Kicks (kick your heels to the backs of your thighs while running).
- Skip/Arm Swing (skip forward while swinging your arms back and forth).
- Toe Kicks (extend one arm straight out in front of you at shoulder level and kick, touching your hand with your toe. Repeat on other side).

Barrieu gives the following tips for getting the most out of warmup stretching:

1. Keep toes pulled up toward your shins to maintain tension in your calves.
2. Keep ground contact time as short as possible—be quick off the ground.
3. Stay on the balls of your feet—don't allow your heels to touch the ground.
4. Work to get full extension in the hips.

After the warm-up, players should spend five or ten minutes on simple soccer moves such as dribbling, passing, and receiving. When players are loose, warm, and soccer-ready, it's time to move on to the drills.

BEST PRACTICES

The best practice sessions are:

- Organized—Coaches should make their practice plans ahead of time and be ready to go the minute players hit the field.

- Purposeful—Coaches should let players know what they are trying to accomplish at each practice. Is there something the team needs to improve upon from the last game?

- Fun—If practice isn't fun, players will lose enthusiasm for the game. Engage players with mini-competitions (as opposed to rote drills) where you keep score and something's at stake—say, the losing team puts the equipment away.

- Flexible—If the coach feels the team has mastered a certain skill or drill, or even if it's just not working on a particular day, move on to something else.

- Fast-Paced—Keep players moving. Even during water breaks, have them "take it on the jog."

- Quiet—Coaches should try not to overtalk. Practice is more productive when players spend the majority of practice time doing, not listening.

DRILLS

Inevitably, drills become part of many soccer practices, especially with players 11 and older. But a lengthy list of long-time coaches agrees that imposing too much structure on young players is a big mistake.

Tony Dicicco, U.S. U-20 Women's National Team coach, discusses this topic in his book, *Catch Them Being Good: Everything You Need to Know to Successfully Coach Girls*: "One thing I hate to see in training is a long line of girls waiting for their turn to go through a maze to practice dribbling. This methodology is totally unnecessary because players can do all the dribbling they need through free movement, where everybody's learning to be aware of space by being creative and improvising. That's how the actual game of soccer is played."

When it comes to players under 11, mostly a coach needs to let his players play and get used to handling the ball. During practice, he should strive to put his players into game-like situations where they can learn by doing.

"You want kids to be purposeful," says Steve Baumann of the National Soccer Hall of Fame. "You want them to think about what they're doing and give them insights into how they should play. You have to put them in situations where positive things happen and they come to know, 'Oh, that's what he meant by that.' So you invent lots of games. For instance, instead of going to one goal at the end of the field, the players run towards two goals. Then if it gets crowded at one goal, we'll move over to the other one. Then the players get it. That's what he means by spreading out!"

So, go ahead and drill your players, but plan carefully. Be sure to keep it moving and have plenty of set-ups going on at once.

TIP FOR COACHES

Among young players, especially those younger than age 6 or 7, practice games with just a few players, three or four, are very popular because each player gets maximum playing time and more opportunities to handle the ball.

JUGGLING

Purpose: To learn ball control by attempting as many touches as possible using any body part except for the hands and arms.

Set-Up: Player begins the solo drill by dropping the ball on her foot, thigh, or head. Next, she pops the ball back into the air and continues juggling it, touching it as many times as possible before it hits the ground.

Variation: Add a partner. Each player takes turns juggling five, ten, or fifteen times before passing the ball.

FIRST-TOUCH PASSING/RECEIVING DRILL

Purpose: To pass and receive using the inside of the foot for the first touch.

Set-Up: Players form four lines and face each other, two lines on each side. The first players in two of the lines pass to the first players in the opposite lines. The receiving players strive to use the inside of the foot with their first touch, then immediately pass the ball back to the player opposite. After passing, each player jogs to the back of the opposite line.

Tip: Receive the ball in as low a position as possible. Strike the ball so it meets the foot on the inside of the shoelaces. Pass with the toe up, and stay over the top of the ball to keep it low.

Variation: Add speed sprints after the pass for more complexity. Have players criss-cross rather than run straight across to practice dodging each other. Then repeat the drill, having players receive the ball with the outside of the foot.

Practice receiving and kicking on the inside and outside of the foot.

FIRST-TOUCH DRIBBLING DRILL

Purpose: To receive the ball by making the first touch on the inside of the foot; then dribble immediately.

Set-Up: Place cones in a straight line down either side of the field. Players line up and move downfield, dribbling around the cones, and then turn and pass the ball back to the next player.

Tip: Lock the ankle. Keep the toe up.

Variation: Players proceed down the field two by two, racing to reach the end line.

5 V 2

Purpose: To practice gaining and keeping possession of the ball and learn how to assist on offense. This exercise combines several skills in one game-like drill.

Set-Up: Place cones in a twelve–by-twelve square. Five players stand on the perimeter of the grid, two defenders stand inside. The perimeter players receive a long kick (from the coach or another player). The receiver dribbles or passes the ball across the grid while teammates try to split the defenders.

Variation: Make the grid larger or smaller. Limit the number of touches allowed to make it more challenging.

CHANGE-OF-DIRECTION DRILL

Purpose: To practice changing direction and beating defenders.

Set-Up: Players form several lines. Players in front start with the ball, dribble 15 yards (13.7 m) to the middle; turn and pass the ball to the next player; then go back to the end of the line. Introduce defenders to the field after two rounds.

Variation: Vary the speed: slow to the middle, then accelerate back. Alternate using the inside and outside of the foot during turns.

TURNING DRILL

Purpose: Learning to shoot or pass after turning.

Set-Up: Place three cones on three corners of a twenty-by-twenty square grid. Three players stand inside the square, then a coach or neutral player kicks the ball toward them. Each player attempts to gain possession of the ball. When one gets possession, she turns and attempts to score by knocking down one of the cones.

Variation: Limit the number of touches allowed before scoring.

GATES GAME

Purpose: To incorporate dribbling, change-of-direction moves, and defense into a fun, game-like competition.

Set-Up: Mark off a twenty-by-twenty square grid. Then, using cones, make six to eight gates (small goals) at different points inside the grid. Divide players into two teams. A team scores when one of its players gets possession of the ball and dribbles through the gate. Defensive players try to block the attackers.

Variation: Make the grid larger or smaller. Change it to a passing game by having players pass through the gate to a waiting teammate to notch a score.

HEAD TO HEAD

Purpose: To practice heading the ball.

Set-Up: Players line up one on one, facing each other, one player on his knees, his partner standing or kneeling across from him. Player #1 tosses the ball up in front of him, then heads it to player #2, who quickly tosses the ball back to him.

Tip: The heading player should arch his back and drive through the ball. He can land on his hands if necessary.

Variation: The standing player tosses the ball to the kneeling player for him to head. Vary the tosses to practice heading balls that hang in the air and balls that come in low.

GOALIE CROSS DRILL

Purpose: For the goalkeeper to practice collecting crosses from both sides.

Set-Up: Two goalies get in position in goals spaced out approximately 40 to 50 yards (36.6 to 45.7 m) apart. Two players position themselves in midfield, one to the right, one to the left. First, the goalkeeper throws a ball to the player standing on the right, who gains control of the ball and pushes it forward before crossing it to the other goalkeeper. The receiving goalkeeper collects the ball and repeats the exercise. Then they repeat the process on the left side.

Variation: Change the distance between the goals.

Note: Try to incorporate the goalkeeper in as many drills as possible. She shouldn't be standing around while her teammates dribble and pass. If there is no role for her in the drill, either put her in with the pack (goalies need to know how to dribble too!) or set up a separate goalie drill.

TIP FOR COACHES

There is an almost unlimited number of drills to use during practice, and there are dozens of sources to seek out ideas and step-by-step how-tos. Check out books such as *101 Great Youth Soccer Drills* by Robert Koger, or surf the Web (http://www.soccerpracticeplans.com, http://www.soccerdrills.com) for ideas. U.S. Youth Soccer's *Coaching Youth Soccer* features an excellent, detailed breakdown of drills by age and skill level.

7: Hey Coach

How to Turn Kids into Players

When they're all grown up, people are often asked who influenced them most when they were young. Besides "my parents," perhaps the number one answer is "my coach." From the mom who just volunteered to coach her 7-year-old's team to the college coach with dozens of wins under his belt, coaching is an enormous privilege, opportunity, and responsibility.

"Coaching is teaching, and teaching is first understanding your student," says National Soccer Hall of Fame president and longtime coach, Steve Baumann. "It's very important that coaches don't come with a preconceived notion of what this particular group of kids can do. The charge of youth coaches is to make each player the best he can be within his own set of talents and skills, then create a way of playing the game that speaks to the strengths of the individuals."

Excellent game plan. But first things first.

WHAT MAKES A GOOD COACH?

Every soccer coach (or manager, as they say in the United Kingdom), is a combination of motivator, cheerleader, tactician, diplomat, role model, friend, teacher, and fellow fan. Anyone who dedicates himself to this task needs to be committed to kids and truly have a love of the game.

According to Jim Thompson, founder of the Positive Coaching Alliance, there are three key ingredients to succeeding as a coach of young players.

1. Be a "double-goal" coach. "Teachable moments present themselves constantly in youth sports, but they are lost if a coach is saddled with a win-at-all-cost mentality. Youth coaches who are not focused on both winning and using sports to teach life lessons should not be coaching kids."

2. Increase players' love of the sport. "A great coach will inspire athletes to love the sport, to want to improve, and to want to come to practice."

A powerful influence.

3. Be an open communicator. "Include players in a conversation about the life of the team. Conversations are more effective than lectures. Ask for suggestions regarding the team's goals, strategies, and tactics, and include players in team decisions."

There are many excellent resources for coaches, including the National Soccer Coaches Association of America (NSCAA), located in Kansas City. The NSCAA counts more than twenty-three thousand members who coach both boys and girls at all levels of the sport. The organization offers coaching education, a national rankings program for colleges and high schools, and an extensive recognition program that offers more than ten thousand awards every year. (See http://www.nscaa.com).

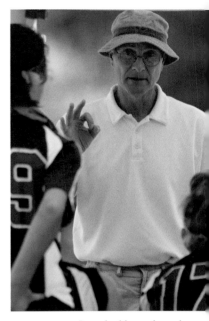

Be a double-goal coach.

U.S. Soccer offers clinics and numerous coaching education materials as well as any certification program a coach may need. Every level of coaching license is available through U.S. Soccer, from the Basic Level "E" Certificate to the Level 3, National "A" licenses. Additional certification programs for more specialized training, such as goalkeeping, fitness, and youth and adult coaching, are also available. (See http://www.ussoccer.com).

"The relationship between player and coach should look like an apprenticeship, where the pupil can spend time with the teacher. Sometimes this can be a scary proposition!"

—MANNY SCHELLSCHEIDT, TECHNICAL DIRECTOR OF U.S. SOCCER'S U-14 BOYS' DEVELOPMENT PROGRAM

Soccer Moms and Dads

The parents of players are an essential part of any successful sports program. But when it comes to soccer, especially the travel leagues where kids play a lot of games, many of them far from home, supportive parents are crucial.

Steve Baumann, president of the National Soccer Hall of Fame and longtime youth coach, used to ask parents of his players the following question at the beginning of every season: "On every soccer field, why is it that the middle of the field has no grass on it and the sides always have a lot of grass? Because that's the place the kids can get farthest away from the parents."

Kidding aside, even parents with the best intentions can find themselves getting in the way of their children's play. But they can also be part of the solution. The parent-coach team is as important as the gaggle of midfielders and fullbacks on each side.

Soccer mom nation: the backbone of the sport.

Accentuate the positive.

CHAMPION THE COACH

Probably the most important thing a parent can do for his soccer player (besides support and encourage the player) is to support the coach. During the practice or game, this means soccer moms and dads need to learn to keep mum and let the coach do the coaching. A young player can easily get overwhelmed with too many people telling her what to do.

According to Baumann, coaches, too, do well to avoid the temptation to talk too much—especially after a mistake on the field. "When I was a player," he says, "every bad pass I ever made in a game, I knew right after I made it that it was bad. I didn't have to be reminded. With kids, you need to be looking ahead. What's the next situation going to be? How can she do better the next time?"

Every coach has to set his own guidelines for working with parents—and, ultimately, every soccer club and league must determine its own philosophy. So there is no confusion, some soccer clubs actually outline expectations for parents' behavior in writing. For a sample Parents Code of Conduct, see Appendix B.

COACH-PARENT PARTNERSHIP[*]

Research shows that when parents and teachers work together, a child tends to do better in school. It's the same in youth sports. The following are some ways parents can contribute to a coach-parent partnership that can help the athlete have the best possible experience.

1. Recognize the commitment the coach has made. For whatever reason, you have chosen not to help coach the team. The coach has made a commitment that involves many, many hours of preparation beyond the hours spent at practices and games. Recognize his commitment and the fact that he is not doing it because of the pay! Try to remember this whenever something goes awry during the season.

2. Make early, positive contact with the coach. As soon as you know who your child's coach is going to be, contact her to introduce yourself and let her know you want to help your child have the best experience she can have this season. To the extent that you can do so, ask if there is any way you can help. If you get to know the coach early and establish a positive relationship, it will be much easier to talk with her later if a problem arises.

3. Fill the coach's emotional tank. When the coach is doing something you like, let him know about it. Coaching is a difficult job, and most coaches only hear from parents when they want to complain about something. This will help fill the coach's emotional tank and help him do a better job. It will also make it easier to raise concerns later if you have shown support for the good things he is doing. And just about every coach does a lot of things well. Take the time to look for them.

4. Don't put the player in the middle. Imagine a situation around the dinner table in which a child's parents complain in front of her about how poorly her math teacher is teaching fractions. How would this impact the student's motivation to work hard to learn fractions? How would it affect her love of mathematics? While this may seem farfetched,

when we move away from school to youth sports, it is all too common for parents to share their disapproval of a coach with their children. This puts a young athlete in a bind. Divided loyalties do not make it easy for a child to do her best. Conversely, when parents support a coach, it is that much easier for the child to put her wholehearted effort into learning to play well. If you think your child's coach is not handling a situation well, do not tell that to the player. Rather, seek a meeting with the coach in which you can talk with her about it.

5. Don't give instructions during a game or practice. You are not one of the coaches, so do not give your child instructions about how to play. It can be very confusing for a child to hear someone other than the coach yelling out instructions during a game. If you have an idea for a tactic, go to the coach and offer it to him. Then let him decide whether he is going to use it or not. If he decides not to use it, let it be. Getting to decide those things is one of the privileges he has earned by making the commitment to coach.

6. Fill your child's emotional tank. Perhaps the most important thing you can do is to be there for your child. Competitive sports are stressful to players, and the last thing they need is a critic at home. Be a cheerleader for your child. Focus on the positive things she is doing, and leave the correcting of mistakes to the coach. Let your player know you support her without reservation regardless of how well she plays.

7. Fill the emotional tanks of the entire team. Cheer for all of the players on the team. Tell each of them when you see them doing something well.

8. Encourage other parents to honor the game. Don't show disrespect for the other team or the officials. But more than that, encourage other parents to honor the game too. If a parent of a player on your team begins to berate the official, gently say, "Hey, that's not honoring the game. That's not the way we do things here."

---

*Courtesy of the Positive Coaching Alliance.

But parents can do a lot more for their player than simply resist the urge
to holler from the sidelines. Soccer moms and dads can get involved.
Offer to help the team by volunteering to:

- Assist the coach
- Run the clock
- Manage equipment
- Organize car pools or phone trees
- Become a referee
- Organize advertising, marketing, and publicity for the team
- Organize a booster club and manage the club's activities
- Assist in making schedules
- Photograph players and games
- Take players to a pro soccer game
- Keep score
- Line the fields
- Chaperone trips
- Set up a team Web site
- Raise funds
- Plan a team party
- Organize coach and player clinics
- Assist during registration
- Create a yearbook or program

Mom's got the stuff.

WHEN A PARENT IS THE COACH

One of the most challenging situations for a parent
(and the player) is when the parent is also his son's
or daughter's coach. Every dad-coach should strive to
treat his child the same way he treats everyone else
on the team. This takes plenty of patience, dedication, and a little creativity. One soccer-mom-turned-
coach of her 8-year-old's team enlisted an assistant, a
father with a child on the team, so they could each
be "in charge" of the other's kid whenever possible.
Another parent-coach cautions never to complain
about games, referees, or other players in front of
your child.

Don't just tell.
Show.

It takes practice for a coach to strike a balance
between not favoring her own child and not being
overly critical of her performance on the field. Equal
treatment is a noble goal, but most parent-coaches
say it's all right to expect more from your child in certain ways. "You
need to hold your own kids to a higher standard of behavior and let
them know you're doing so," said Ijamsville, Maryland, youth coach
Tim Gipson. "Explain to them the need to be a good example. Kids
like to lead when given the chance. But do not hold them to a higher
standard regarding their play."

"I tried to treat my boys the same as any other kid, but I know
I demanded more," said Doug Taylor, a youth coach in Chesterfield,
Virginia, for nine years. "Not that they had to be the best players on
the team, but they had to be leaders. They had to set an example, try

harder, be where they were supposed to be, and help get the kids and the equipment organized."

With a little thought and planning, coaching your own child can be an incredibly memorable and rewarding experience.

TIP FOR COACHES

"Even if you have never played soccer before, new coaches shouldn't feel intimidated, especially at the recreational level, where kids are there because they want to participate and have fun. There are many resources out there. Attend clinics. Check out the Internet. And be sure to invite more experienced players to come to practice to demonstrate skills for younger players. Showing them what to do is so much more effective than telling them what to do."—*Coach Trip Ellis, FC Richmond*

Patience pays.

HITTING THE FIELD

TESTING 1-2-3

At the start of every season, it's important for a soccer coach to evaluate his players. What are their skills? Where do they need more work? What should their goals be? A coach of more advanced players will want to take an additional step and evaluate her players' fitness and skill level more closely. Once she has done this, she will be well equipped to assign positions and put together a game plan. A coach may also use tests or assessments throughout the year or at the end of a season to determine team placement for the following year.

Some valuable tests include the following.

Keep it up.

JUGGLING

A player juggles the ball using both feet, the body, and the head for as many consecutive touches as possible. This is a great way to determine if a player has been practicing essential skills on her own.

Some clubs set goals for the number of juggling touches according to age. Here is a sample chart:

U-10	50
U-11	100
U-12	200
U-13	300
U-14	400
U-15	500
U-16	600
U-17	700
U-18	800

THE BEEP TEST

This evaluation of a player's cardiovascular fitness is also known as the "Multi-Stage Fitness Test," the "pacer test," or the "shuttle run test." First, 22-yard (20-meter) lanes are set up, with two cones at either end to create gates. The runner stands at one end while a teammate or coach stands nearby to keep score. The coach starts a recording that plays continuous beeps at set intervals, signaling the runner to go. The runner's goal is to reach the opposite gate before the next beep sounds. Each stage of the test lasts approximately sixty seconds and gets progressively more challenging, with beeps closer together. (See Appendix C.)

T-Test

This test measures speed and agility by clocking the time it takes a player to complete a course that includes forward, lateral, and backward running. For this test, the coach will need a stopwatch and a helper to serve as a spotter. (See Appendix D.)

Manchester United Fitness Test

Youth and high school coaches often provide extra incentive by using tests borrowed from famous teams. Many of these tests and other resources (such as training exercises) are available through the teams' Web sites or simply by requesting copies of their training packets.

The pressure is on.

The Manchester United evaluation allows coaches to assess speed and endurance by assigning a level to each player after she does a series of one-minute 100-yard (91.4-m) runs, sprinting up and jogging back. (See Appendix E.)

U.S. Women's National Team Battery of Tests

Who can argue with the success of the U.S. Women's team? Their record speaks for itself, and many coaches borrow from their testing/ training program. The ten tests listed in their training guide include several commonly used by coaches at all levels to measure muscular endurance and speed, as well as more sophisticated tests for measuring an athlete's transfer of horizontal and vertical power and balance. (See Appendix F for a description of the Vertical Jump Test.)

Advice for the first-time coach from World Cup champion turned U.S. Soccer U-17 coach Wilmer Cabrera: "You only have to give players confidence and possibilities and make them have fun. Show them that they can have fun and be competitive and that they can trust what they have. That's the way I learned."

PRACTICE PLAN

In the early 1990s, researchers at Michigan State University's Youth Sports Institute polled a group of young players who had dropped out of sports and asked them what would make them want to play again. The number one response? "If practices were more fun."

Kids of every age want to be active, especially young ones, so the better organized a coach is with his practice plan, the less time players will spend standing around and the more fun they'll have at practice. Jim Thompson recommends that every practice consist of the following:

- An opening ritual to signify the transition to being with the team
- Team conversations in which the coach engages the players in team business as opposed to standing up to lecture
- Instruction in new skills and tactics
- Conditioning
- Scrimmaging
- Drills and activities that remind players what fun it is to play soccer
- Discussion of a life lesson in which the coach relates what was learned in practice to other parts of the players' lives
- A closing ritual that sends players off with a positive feeling

SAFETY FIRST

The first priority of every coach in any sport should be the safety of her players. Her first order of business should be to make sure that every player wears properly fitting shoes and shin guards and that the goalkeeper (if older than 12) wears gloves and other pads.

Since a player can get hurt just as easily during practice as he can during a game, the coach needs to enforce safety rules on practice days the same way a referee would on game day. Coaches should be sure to complete first aid and CPR training provided by a nationally recognized organization such as the American Red Cross or the National Safety Council. (Many leagues make this mandatory.) Also, every coach must keep a list of emergency numbers and a well-stocked first aid kit on hand.

The first aid kit should include the following items:

- Cell phone
- Mirror
- Disposable plastic gloves
- Triangular bandages
- Adhesive tape
- Cotton balls
- Saline solution
- Peroxide
- Hydrocortisone cream
- Safety pins
- Plastic bags (for ice)
- Flashlight
- Scissors
- Roll gauze
- Square gauze pads
- Band-aids (all sizes)
- Tongue depressors
- Antibacterial soap
- Insect sting kit
- Thermometer

Just as important as a well-stocked first aid kit is a well-thought-out emergency plan. Coaches may ask for a volunteer committee of parents to help organize the team's emergency plan, which should include creating an emergency response card that contains phone numbers and medical information for each athlete and spelling out how the team will deal with minor and major injuries.

Sum it up before you send 'em home.

P-R-I-C-E

According to the American Sport Education Program, coaches should use the **PRICE** method to aid an injured player.

P—Protect the athlete and injured body part from further danger or trauma.

R—Rest the area to avoid further damage and foster healing.

I—Ice the area to reduce swelling and pain.

C—Compress the area by securing an ice bag in place with an elastic wrap.

E—Elevate the injury above heart level to keep the blood from pooling in the area.

> **"When it comes to coaching a youngster, the bottom line should always be that the child have fun. If your daughter comes home, goes to the backyard, and starts kicking the ball around, you know that the coach has done a great job."**
>
> —TONY DICICCO, COACH OF THE 1996 OLYMPIC GOLD MEDAL AND 1999 WORLD CUP CHAMPION U.S. WOMEN'S NATIONAL TEAM

> **Understand people first, then worry about the X's and O's."**—UNIVERSITY OF FLORIDA AND NCAA CHAMPIONSHIP COACH BECKY BURLEIGH

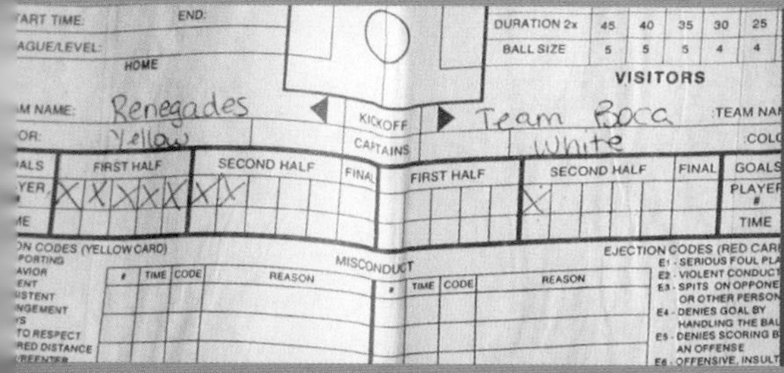

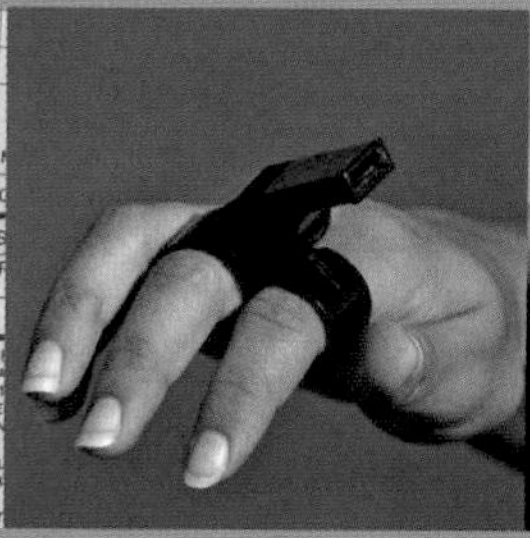

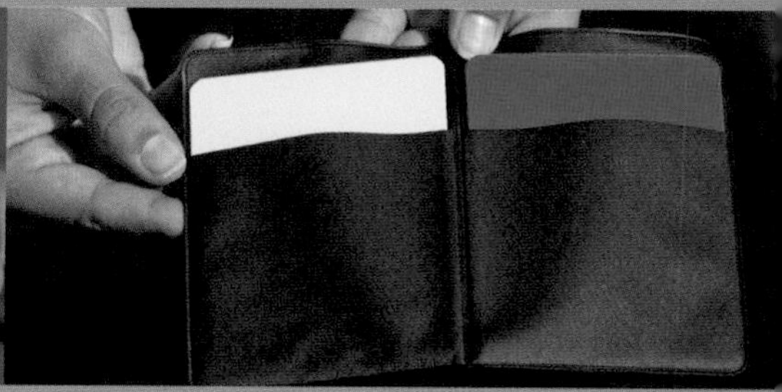

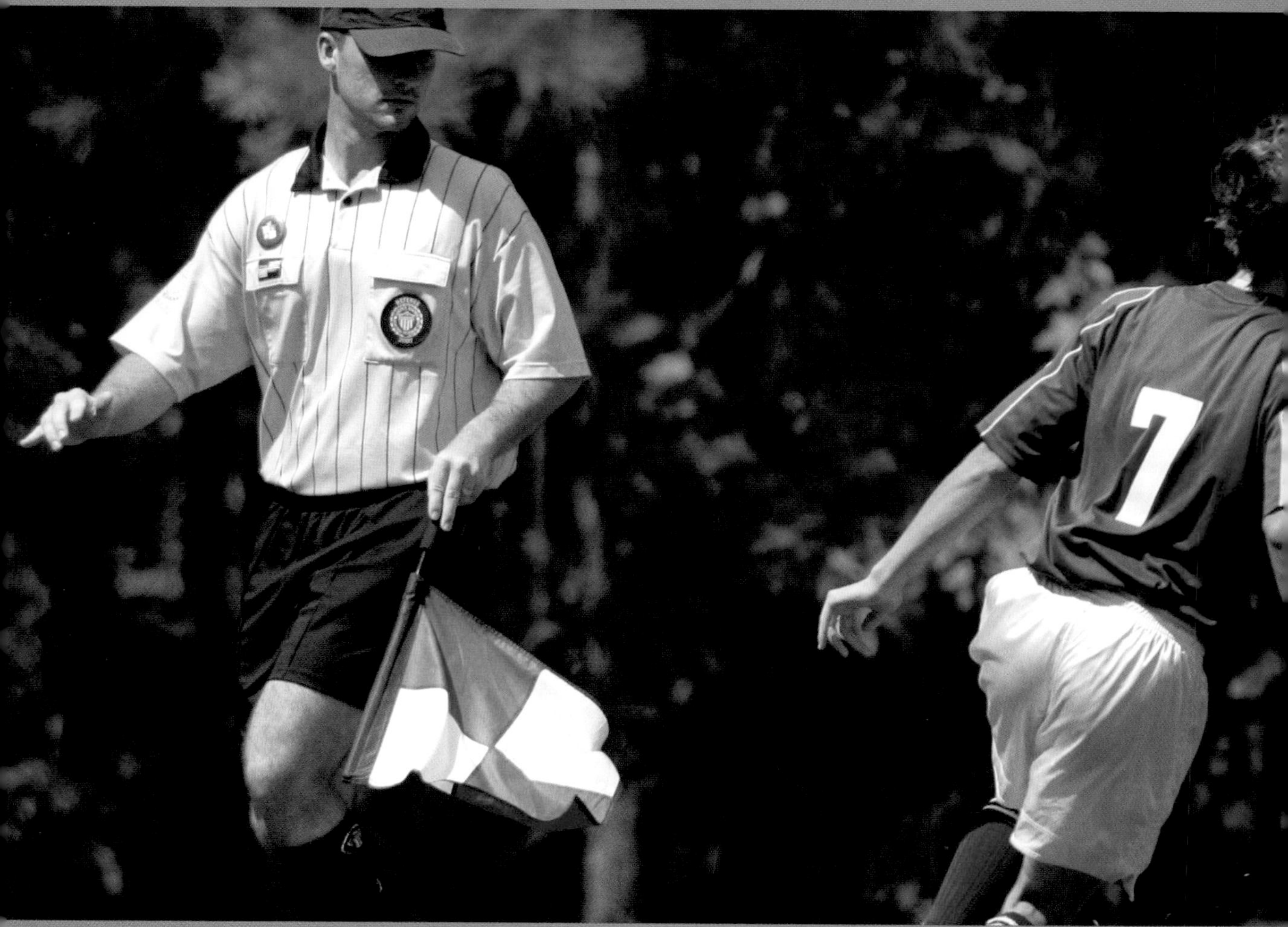

8: Make It Official

How to Keep Score, Keep It Safe, and Keep the Match Moving

Centuries ago, there were no rules in soccer. According to one British historian, before the *Laws of the Game* were written, men used soccer as an excuse for "an uninhibited ruck." These days, rules are enforced so players have fun but still stay safe.

Referees are an important cog in the soccer machine. None of the matches taking place all over the world every weekend could be played without officials to make the calls. At the youth level, referees are mostly volunteers who care enough about the players to get involved. At the college and pro levels, referees are often former players who aren't ready to hang up their boots.

As many refs say, when no one notices them, they've done a good job. So, what does it take to effectively operate under the radar? Officially?

WHAT DO REFS DO?

The main job of the referee is to control the match. He is the chief official and timekeeper. He enforces the *Laws of the Game* and, using his trusty flags and cards, calls all fouls, and starts and stops play. All decisions of the referee are final. And players, coaches, and parents challenge the ref at their peril!

The youngest players (usually age 6 and under) often play without referees; if they do use a referee, there will be just one official on the field. Under-10 players usually have two referees on the field, while at older players' games, it's common to see a referee joined by two or even three assistants.

Procedures and policies vary between leagues, so new referees should always check with their district administrator to find out how things work.

Get by with a little help from your friends.

A Little Help

Since the center (or main) referee can't be everywhere and see everything, two assistant referees (linesmen) also work the field during older players' matches. The assistants are charged with signaling the following:

- When the ball goes out of bounds
- When a team is awarded a corner kick, throw-in, or goal kick
- When a player is in an offside position
- When a substitution is requested
- When misconduct or any other incident occurs outside the referee's view or where an assistant is closer to the action than the referee
- During a penalty kick, whether the goalkeeper moved forward before kicking the ball and whether the ball crosses the goal line

Flags flying.

Note: It's easy to identify which is which—linesmen stand on the sidelines and signal with flags. Center referees take the middle of the field and signal with their hands and their whistles.

Stops and Starts

One of the most important things a referee does is to determine when the game should stop and start again. Since soccer is a free-flowing game, every referee does her best to stop play only when it is absolutely necessary. Besides the stoppages the rules require—for certain fouls and when a goal is scored or a ball goes out of bounds—refs

Time to make a switch.

should stop the match only when some sort of outside interference has occurred or when a player is seriously injured. Officials may use their judgment regarding slightly injured players, either calling for a substitution or allowing the player to continue playing in the match. That said, the *Laws of the Game* state that any player bleeding from a wound must leave the field and may return only after the bleeding has stopped and he has received a signal from the referee.

Another potentially game-stopping situation is when a player is called offside. Basically, a player is in the offside position when she is closer to her opponents' goal than both the ball and two opposing players at the moment the ball is played by a teammate. An exception is made when a player is on her own half of the field or on the opponents' half but either level with the last defender or receiving the ball directly from a goal kick, throw-in, or corner kick.

In the interest of keeping the game moving, a player is only called offside if the referee believes the player gained an unfair advantage or interfered with play or with an opponent.

Penalty for offside: An indirect free kick is awarded to the opposing team.

"Offside" is a two-part call.

ALL EYES ON THE REF

As a fan, it's tempting to keep your eye trained on the ball or the players in the middle of the action. But watching the ref is the only way to know what's really going on game-wise. Here's a cheat sheet of what to watch (and listen) for.

Keep your whistle handy.

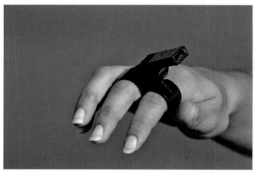

WHISTLE

When the ref blows his whistle, something (usually a foul) has occurred on the field to stop the game:

- Short, quick whistle: Indicates a lesser foul punishable by a free kick
- Longer, louder whistle: Indicates a serious foul punishable by cards or penalty kicks

Bring on the Sheriff: England's Nottingham Forest club introduced the first referee's whistle in 1878.

ADVANTAGE

If the ref extends both arms out to her sides, she just saw a foul but is waiting (usually just a few seconds) to determine which team appears to have benefited from what occurred. If an advantage (such as possession kept or a goal scored) is gained by the fouled team, she will ignore the foul and allow play to continue. If the foul warranted a card, however, the ref will show the card at the next stoppage in play.

CORNER KICK

When the referee points at the corner flag, he is signaling for a corner kick. This is awarded to the attacking team after the defending team clears the ball over the end or goal line.

Note: If the linesman makes the call, he points with his flag. If the center referee makes the call, he points with his hand.

"Every referee gets the chance to make seventy or more decisions during every game."—DAVE HILLEND, DISTRICT REFEREE ADMINISTRATOR, CORAL SPRINGS, FLORIDA

Direct Free Kick (DFK)

When the referee blows her whistle and points with a raised arm in the direction of the offending player's goal, she is signaling for a direct free kick. A DFK is awarded when a player kicks, trips, charges, jumps at, strikes, pushes, or holds an opponent. DFKs are also awarded when a player handles the ball with his hands or, while attempting to tackle the opponent, makes contact with the opponent before touching the ball. Note: The defending team must stand at least 10 yards (9.1 m) away from the ball prior to the kick. A goal may be scored from a DFK.

Goal Kick

When the referee points at the goal with his arm pointed straight, parallel to the ground, he is signaling for a goal kick. The goalkeeper takes this kick after the attacking team shoots the ball over the end line. (Note: If a linesman makes the call, he uses a flag to point toward the goal. The center referee points with his hand.)

INDIRECT FREE KICK (IFK)

If after signaling for a free kick the referee keeps her hand above her head, then she is calling for an indirect free kick. Note: She will keep her hand up until after the ball has been kicked, then touched by another player. An IFK is awarded if a player performs in a dangerous way, obstructs an opponent, or stops the goalkeeper from releasing the ball from his hands. A goalie may be called for an IFK if he takes more than four steps before releasing the ball, touches the ball with his hands after it has been thrown or kicked by a teammate, or wastes time. Note: A goal may be scored from an IFK, but only after it has touched one other player in addition to the shooter.

PENALTY KICK

When the referee points directly to the penalty spot, or the spot two-thirds of the way between the penalty area line and goal area line, he is indicating that a player committed a foul in the penalty area and a penalty kick will be taken there. Only the goalkeeper stands between the net and the shooter.

IN THE CARDS

Every referee keeps two cards in her kit—one red, one yellow—that are used only for the most serious offenses. Think of them in terms of a traffic light: Yellow means caution; red means stop. Ideally, if players are playing a safe and fair match, the ref can keep her cards close to the vest.

YELLOW CARD

A ref shows a yellow card to indicate that a player has committed a dangerous action such as kicking an opponent, handling the ball, or dissenting (disagreeing with a game official). Two yellow cards equal one red card, which means automatic ejection from the game.

RED CARD

When a ref awards a red card, it means the recipient has committed a serious or violent action on the field, such as tackling from behind, a vicious kick, or spitting, and must leave the field immediately.

FOUL CALLS

FOULS THAT WARRANT A DIRECT FREE KICK

- Kicking or attempting to kick an opponent
- Tripping or attempting to trip an opponent
- Jumping at an opponent
- Charging an opponent
- Striking or attempting to strike an opponent
- Pushing an opponent
- When tackling an opponent to gain possession of the ball, making contact with the opponent before touching the ball
- Holding an opponent
- Spitting at an opponent
- Handling the ball deliberately

FOULS THAT WARRANT AN INDIRECT FREE KICK

- The goalkeeper fails to release the ball within six seconds.
- The goalkeeper touches the ball with a hand after releasing it and before it is touched by another player.
- The goalkeeper touches the ball with his hands after receiving it from a teammate's kick.
- The goalkeeper touches the ball with his hands after receiving it from a teammate's throw-in.
- Playing in a dangerous manner.

- Impeding the progress of an opponent.
- Preventing the goalkeeper from releasing the ball from his hands.
- Any other offense for which play is stopped to caution a player or send her off the field.

YELLOW CARD (CAUTION) OFFENSES

- Unsporting behavior
- Showing dissent by word or action
- Persistent infringement of the *Laws of the Game*
- Delaying the restart of play
- Failing to respect the required distance when play is restarted with a corner kick or free kick or throw-in
- Entering or re-entering the field of play without the referee's permission
- Deliberately leaving the field of play without the referee's permission

RED CARD (SENDING OFF) OFFENSES

- Serious foul play
- Violent conduct
- Spitting at any person
- Denying the opposing team a goal or an obvious goal-scoring opportunity by deliberately handling the ball. (A goalkeeper within her own penalty area is exempt.)
- Denying an obvious goal-scoring opportunity to an opponent moving toward the player's goal by an offense punishable by a free kick or a penalty kick.
- Offensive, insulting, or abusive language and/or gestures.
- Two cautions (yellow cards) in the same match.

TIP FOR PLAYERS, PARENTS, AND COACHES

Do not ever attempt to challenge the referee, no matter what. During a soccer match, the referee's calls are always right, no matter how wrong they may be. Challenging the ref may result in being shown a yellow or even a red card.

The ref is always right.

GET IN GEAR

With apologies to Johnny Cash—and Will Smith and Tommy Lee Jones—referees used to be known as "The Men in Black," since that was the only color officials were allowed to wear during soccer matches. Then, in the early 1980s, some pro teams began wearing black uniforms. Obviously, this presented a problem, so FIFA changed the rules. In 1999, U.S. Soccer designated the official national referee uniform to consist of a gold jersey with black pinstripes, black collar, black cuffs (long sleeves) or no cuff (short sleeves), black shorts, black socks, and black shoes. Alternates' jerseys are black and red.

In youth soccer, uniform rules vary from league to league. Often, referees will keep several shirts on hand and coordinate with the assistant referees to wear the most appropriate color depending on the match to stand out from the players. New refs should contact the league referee administrator for what to wear and where to buy uniforms and supplies.

Suited up.

TOOLS OF THE TRADE

Many leagues supply equipment such as timers or substitution signs. Here is a basic list of the other supplies a ref will need to do his job:

UNIFORM

■ Referee shirt (usually yellow; other colors include red, blue, green, and black)

■ Shorts

■ Badge or patch

■ Cap

■ Comfortable black turf shoes or cleats

■ Knee socks

■ Rain gear

EQUIPMENT

■ Gear bag

■ Bag for wet shoes/clothes

■ Flag set

■ Cards (red and yellow)

■ Whistle and lanyard

■ Score pad (waterproof or water resistant)

■ Pen/marker

■ Flip coin

■ Countdown timer

■ Watch

Keeping score.

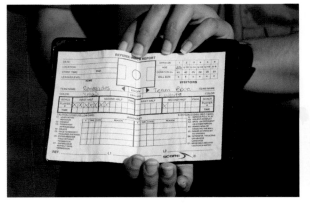

Cards—just in case.

GETTING STARTED

So, you want to make it official? The first step is to contact U.S. Soccer or the American Youth Soccer Organization (AYSO) to find out the name of the referee administrator in your state. This person (or referee liaisons at U.S. Soccer and AYSO) can outline the procedure for getting licensed and direct you to training in your district. Note: Many referees get certified by both groups. These organizations, as well as other officials in your local league, are a great resource for upcoming clinics and work opportunities. U.S. Soccer's Web site includes everything from detailed Q&As on game situations to a full fitness program for referees.

U.S. Soccer lists over 150,000 registered referees—including instructors and assessors—calling games at every level of the sport in the United States, including youth, amateur, professional, and sanctioned international competitions.

Advantage rule: A clause in the rules that allows the referee to refrain from stopping play for a foul if doing so would benefit the team that committed the violation.

Carrying the ball: A foul called on a goalkeeper when he takes more than four steps while holding or bouncing the ball.

Caution: *see Yellow card.*

Direct free kick: A kick awarded to a player for a serious foul committed by the opposition; the player kicks a stationary ball with no opposing players within 10 yards (9.1 m) of him; a goal can be scored directly from this kick without the ball touching another player.

Drop ball: A method of restarting a game where the referee drops the ball between two players facing each other.

Foul: A violation of the rules for which an official assesses a free kick.

Free kick: A kick awarded to a player for a foul committed by the opposition; the player kicks a stationary ball without any opposing players within 10 yards (9.1 m) of him.

Goal kick: A type of restart in which the ball is kicked from inside the goal area away from the goal; awarded to the defending team when a ball that crossed the goal line was last touched by a player on the attacking team.

Hacking: Kicking an opponent's legs.

Hand ball: A foul in which a player touches the ball with his hand or arm; the opposing team is awarded a direct free kick.

In bounds: When a ball is within the boundaries of the field, having not completely crossed a sideline or goal line.

In play: When a ball is within the boundaries of the field and play has not been stopped by the referee.

Indirect free kick: A kick awarded to a player for a less serious foul committed by the opposition; the player kicks a stationary ball without any opposing players within 10 yards (9.1 m) of him; a goal can be scored on this kick only after the ball has touched another player.

Injury time: Time added to the end of any period according to the referee's judgment of time lost due to player injuries or intentional stalling by a team.

Linesmen: The two officials who assist the referee in making his decisions; they monitor the sidelines and goal lines to determine when a ball goes out of bounds; they carry flags to signal their observations.

Official game clock: The clock that the referee carries with him on the field so he can signal when each half is over; it does not stop during the game, even when play does.

Officials: The referee and two linesmen (and, at the highest level of play, the fourth official) who work together to make sure the game is played according to the rules of soccer; responsible for stopping and restarting play, keeping track of the score and the time remaining, and citing violations of the rules, called fouls; they wear uniforms that distinguish them from the players on both teams.

Offside: A violation called when a player in an offside position receives a pass from a teammate; an indirect free kick is awarded to the non-offending team.

Offside position: An attacking player positioned so that fewer than two opposing defensive players (usually the goalie and one other defender) are between him and the goal he is attacking; a player is not offside if he is exactly even with one or both of these defensive players.

Onside: The opposite of offside.

Out of bounds: When a ball is outside the boundaries of the field, having completely crossed a sideline or goal line.

Out of play: When a ball is outside the boundaries of the field or play has been stopped by the referee.

Penalty: Short for penalty kick; also, a punishment given by the referee for a violation of the rules.

Penalty arc: A circular arc whose center is the penalty spot and extends from the top of the penalty area; designates an area that opposing players are not allowed to enter prior to a penalty kick.

Penalty area: A rectangular area 44 yards (40.2 m) wide by 18 yards (16.5 m) deep with its long edge on the goal line; the goalkeeper may use his hands to block or control the ball only within this area.

Penalty kick (or penalty shot): A kick taken from the penalty spot by a player against the opposing goalie without any players closer than 10 yards (9.1 m) away; awarded for the most severe rule violations and those committed by the defense within its own penalty area; also taken in a tiebreaker to decide a match.

Penalty spot: The small circular spot located 12 yards (11.0 m) in front of the center of the goal line from which all penalty kicks are taken; positioned at the center of the penalty arc.

Play on: A term used by referees to indicate that no foul or stoppage is to be called; used by referees when applying the Advantage Rule.

Professional foul: A foul committed intentionally, usually by a defender on an attacker just outside the defender's penalty area; used to prevent a scoring opportunity without incurring a penalty shot.

Red card: A card (approximately the size of a playing card) that a referee holds up to signal a player's removal from the game; presented for violent behavior or multiple rule infractions (two yellow cards = one red card); the player's team must play the rest of the game shorthanded.

Shoulder charge: Minimal shoulder-to-shoulder contact by a defender against a ball carrier; the only contact allowed by the rules unless a defender touches the ball first.

Timekeeper: The job of the referee, who keeps track of the official time to notify teams and fans when each period is completed.

Time-out: An official break in the action of a sport; the rules of soccer do not allow for any time-outs; time-outs for television advertising breaks are permitted by NCAA collegiate rules.

Unsportsmanlike conduct: Rude or bad behavior such as kicking a player when he is on the ground, throwing equipment, or arguing with the referee.

Yellow card: A card that a referee holds up to warn a player for dangerous or unsportsmanlike behavior; also called a "caution"; two yellow cards in one game earns a player an automatic red card, signaling his removal from the game.

APPENDIXES

APPENDIX A: INDIVIDUAL PRESEASON FITNESS PROGRAM[*]

The more fit players are when they come into preseason team training, the less time will be spent on fitness!

The fitness program should take about an hour each day. The first 30 minutes will be the same every day, followed by a long program or a short program on alternating days. Testing will be conducted during the first few days of preseason training to assess each player's fitness.

It is very important to complete all stretching and warm-up exercises BEFORE and AFTER all sessions included in this training program. With proper stretching, the incidence of muscle injury can be greatly reduced. Proper intake of water and a good diet are essential. Also, each player should try to get into a consistent sleep pattern. All of these factors will help improve performance on the field.

WARM-UP

It is imperative to properly warm up your body to prepare it for the demands of the workout and to reduce your risk of injury.

_____

*Courtesy of FC Richmond (Richmond, Virginia)

Start off each session with:

1. Light jogging, skipping, side-to-side running—6 minutes.
2. Stretching—4 minutes. Stretch the quadriceps (front of the thigh), hamstrings (back of the thigh), calves (back of the lower leg), groin (inner part of the upper thigh), back, arms, neck, etc.
3. Juggling—10 minutes. Each day try to beat your previous juggling record, using only one body part (foot, thigh, head, etc.). Juggle with a partner and perform one-touch, two-touch, and various games and competitions. Below are juggling targets for different age groups.

U-10	50
U-11	100
U-12	200
U-13	300
U-14	400
U-15	500
U-16	600
U-17	700
U-18	800

4. Coerver—10 minutes. Practice fast footwork moves, getting as many touches on the ball as possible, one-touch passing against a wall, with a partner, etc.

RUNNING PROGRAM

After the 30-minute warm-up phase, the middle of each training session is devoted to running—either a long run (distance and pace depending on players' age) or a series of short runs ("shuttles"). Here are some ways to vary the workout on short-run days:

1. Run backwards.

2. Run with the ball, stopping it on the line each time.

3. Start with the last cone first and work your way back.

COOL-DOWN

Just as warming up your body for training is essential, it is equally important to cool down after your workout to prevent injuries and to help rid your muscles of lactic acid build up. End each session with:

1. Light jogging, skipping, shaking the legs out, etc.—5 minutes.

2. Stretching—4 minutes. Stretch the quadriceps, hamstrings, calves, groin, back, arms, neck, etc.

3. Strength—6 minutes.

    U14 – U19 200 crunches/sit-ups, 100 push-ups 50 leg raises

    U10 – U13 100 crunches/sit-ups, 50 push-ups, 25 leg raises

4. Juggling—up to 5 minutes.

FITNESS SCHEDULE

DAY 1: WARM-UP
U15–U19 long run 3 miles (4.8 km) at 8 minute pace
U10–U14 long run 2 miles (3.2 km) at 9 minute pace
Cool-down

DAY 2: WARM-UP
Short run (shuttles): Set 5 markers from starting point 5 yards (4.6 m) apart (25 yards [22.9 m] total)
U15–U19 complete < 38 seconds
U10–U14 complete < 45 seconds
All: 5 repetitions with 2 minutes of rest between each
Cool-down

DAY 3: WARM-UP

U15–U19 long run 3 miles (4.8 km) at 8 minute pace

U10–U14 long run 2 miles (3.2 km) at 9 minute pace

Cool-down

DAY 4: WARM-UP

Shuttles: Set 5 markers from starting point 5 yards (4.6 m) apart

U15–U19 complete < 38 seconds

U10–U14 complete < 45 seconds

All: 6 repetitions with 2 minutes of rest between each

Cool-down

DAY 5: WARM-UP

U15–U19 Long run 3 miles (4.8 km) at 7 minute pace

U10–U14 Long run 2 miles (3.2 km) at 8 minute pace

Cool-down

DAY 6: WARM-UP

Shuttles: Set 5 markers from starting point 5 yards (4.6 m) apart

U15–U19 complete < 38 seconds

U10–U14 complete < 45 seconds

All: 7 repetitions with 2 minutes of rest between each

Cool-down

DAY 7: REST DAY

DAY 8: WARM-UP

U15–U19 long run 3 miles (4.8 km) at 7 minute pace

U10–U14 long run 2 miles (3.2 km) at 8 minute pace

Cool-down

DAY 9: WARM-UP

Shuttles: Set 5 markers from starting point 5 yards (4.6 m) apart

U15–U19 complete < 38 seconds

U10–U14 complete < 45 seconds

All: 8 repetitions with 2 minutes of rest between each

Cool-down

DAY 10: WARM-UP

U15–U19 long run 3 miles (4.8 km) at 7 minute pace

U10–U14 long run 2 miles (3.2 km) at 8 minute pace

Cool-down

DAY 11: WARM-UP

Shuttles: Set 5 markers from starting point 5 yards (4.6 m) apart

U15–U19 complete < 38 seconds

U10–U14 complete < 45 seconds

All: 9 repetitions with 2 minutes of rest between each

Cool-down

DAY 12: WARM-UP

U15–U19 long run 3 miles (4.8 km) at 6 minute pace

U10–U14 long run 2 miles (3.2 km) at 7 minute pace

Cool-down

DAY 13: REST DAY

DAY 14: TEAM TRAINING BEGINS

APPENDIX B: PARENTS' CODE OF CONDUCT[*]

Parents must conduct themselves properly at all times, on and off the soccer field, while representing the club. Inflammatory language, profane remarks or gestures, and derogatory remarks regarding gender, race, religion, or country of origin will not be tolerated.

Parents should:

- Stay on the spectators' side before and during games. Once a player arrives at the field for the game, he/she is under the direction of the coach.
- Wait on the spectators' side after the game. Players will dress on the sidelines (change jersey and shoes) and then come across the field to the parents.
- Applaud good play by either team.
- Understand that players, coaches, and referees (like everyone else) learn by making mistakes.
- Talk to their team manager as soon as they have any concerns or questions.
- Never approach coaches before, during, or after games.
- Never coach from the sidelines.
- Always contact coaches or Directors of Coaching through proper communication channels.
- Never yell at the referee or players. (If you can't control your emotions, either stop going to the games or stand so far away from the field that no one else can hear you.)
- Never criticize players, coaches, or referees to their children or to other parents.

Parents help their children achieve the best possible playing experience when they cooperate with coaches and referees. It's an easy thing to do when everyone remembers their common goal: a positive, fun experience for the players.

---

*Courtesy of FC Richmond (Richmond, Virginia)

Appendix C: Beep Test

Warm-Up

- Before the endurance test begins, players should warm-up and stretch.

Set-Up

- On flat ground or turf, section off one 22-yard (20-m) lane for every two players to be tested. Place two cones on the ground at each end to mark a shoulder-width gate.
- One player, the recorder, stands at the end of the lane to keep score.
- The other player, the runner, stands at the opposite end of the lane (facing the recorder).

Procedure

- After the warm-up and set-up, the coach should explain the test to the players and, using a CD (with pre-recorded beeps), allow the players to run a few repetitions at the lowest speed so that they become familiar with the two sounds on the CD.
- A single beep is used to indicate the start and stop of each interval. The first beep starts the runner, the next one signals the end of the first interval and the start of the next.

Runner Instructions

- At the start, the player must have one foot between the two cones that define the gate on one end of the lane.
- At each beep from the recording, the player must run to the gate at the opposite end and get a foot between the cones at that opposite end gate before the next beep sounds.
- If the runner does not arrive early enough to place a foot in the cone gate, that is, on the imaginary line connecting the two cones, a miss will be recorded.
- Two misses in a row retires the runner from the test.

Recorder Instructions

- The recorder, holding a beep test record form (at right) and pen, keeps track by marking through the number corresponding to the repetition number at each speed as the runner completes the interval successfully.

- The recorder marks along each row, from left to right, until the runner completes all repetitions at that speed.

- When all repetitions for a running speed are completed, the recorder moves down to the next row.

- If the runner arrives late, the recorder circles the repetition as "failed" and warns the runner by saying, "Warning!"

- If the runner misses two gates in a row, the runner is retired. Note: Missing two gates does not force the runner to retire, only missing two *consecutive* gates.

Coach Instructions

- Ensure that the course is accurately measured to confirm the value and comparability of the results.

- Ensure that the recorders understand the instructions.

- Ensure that the runners who arrive early at the end of the gate wait until the beep to return to the other end.

- Note that at the lower speeds, players might be laughing or complaining about the ease of the test. However, things get quiet at about speed 9, and by speed 11 or 13, players begin to drop out. (The test may have up to twenty-three levels.)

BEEP TEST

Photocopy this chart for use on the field.

Level One

Player's Name:

Date:

Speed

1	1	2	3	4	5	6	7								
2	1	2	3	4	5	6	7	8							
3	1	2	3	4	5	6	7	8							
4	1	2	3	4	5	6	7	8							
5	1	2	3	4	5	6	7	8	9						
6	1	2	3	4	5	6	7	8	9						
7	1	2	3	4	5	6	7	8	9	10					
8	1	2	3	4	5	6	7	8	9	10					
9	1	2	3	4	5	6	7	8	9	10	11				
10	1	2	3	4	5	6	7	8	9	10	11				
11	1	2	3	4	5	6	7	8	9	10	11				
12	1	2	3	4	5	6	7	8	9	10	11	12			
13	1	2	3	4	5	6	7	8	9	10	11	12			
14	1	2	3	4	5	6	7	8	9	10	11	12	13		
15	1	2	3	4	5	6	7	8	9	10	11	12	13		
16	1	2	3	4	5	6	7	8	9	10	11	12	13		
17	1	2	3	4	5	6	7	8	9	10	11	12	13	14	
18	1	2	3	4	5	6	7	8	9	10	11	12	13	14	
19	1	2	3	4	5	6	7	8	9	10	11	12	13	14	15
20	1	2	3	4	5	6	7	8	9	10	11	12	13	14	15

Mark a line through each repetition completed along the row for each speed. Circle the misses. Please note: When the runner misses two in a row, he is retired.

APPENDIX D: T-TEST

Coach

- Set up four cones in a "T" formation (three across the top, spaced 5 yards [4.6 m] apart, one below, spaced 10 yards [9.1 m] away from the top three) on the field or on an indoor surface of 11 yards square (10 m square). (Note: Cone B should be slightly staggered so players don't topple it running back across).

C B D

A

- Assign a spotter to stand 3 yards (2.7 m) behind cone A to catch players in case they fall while running backward.
- Instruct players to warm up for five to ten minutes.

Player

- Start with one hand and the opposite foot on the start line (cone A). If a touch pad is used, the lead hand must be on the pad. From cone A, sprint forward to cone B, and touch the base of it with your right hand.
- Facing forward without crossing your feet, shuffle left to cone C, and touch its base with your left hand.
- Shuffle right to cone D, and touch its base with your right hand.
- Shuffle back to cone B, and touch it with your left hand.
- Run backward as quickly as possible past cone A to the finish.

The test score is the best time of three trials. Note: Players who cross one foot in front of the other, fail to touch the base of the cones, or fail to face forward throughout the test should be disqualified.

APPENDIX E: MANCHESTER UNITED FITNESS TEST (MODIFIED)

This test is also known as "Full Field Sprints."

Goal: Test players' running fitness.

Set-up: Place two cones 100 yards (91.4 m) apart.

Test: Runners sprint the length of the field (from cone to cone) and jog back at a predetermined pace.

Total time each run: One minute.

Pace: Begin with ten identical runs (levels 1–10). Difficulty increases at each subsequent level (11 and up).

NOTE: Begin with five-minute warm-up. End with five-minute cool down.

RUN (LEVEL)	PACED TIME (IN SECONDS)	RECOVERY TIME (IN SECONDS)
1–10	24	36
11	23	37
12	22	38
13	21	39
14	20	40
15	19	41
16	18	42
17	17	43
18	16	44
19	15	45
20–30	15	45

RECOVERY TIME is a slow jog back to the original starting line. The next run begins at the one-minute mark.

Your LEVEL is the last PACED TIME that you managed. You have to make each paced time run within the time allowed. (For example, if you fail to make the 22-second PACED TIME, you are at LEVEL 12.)

Suggestion: In order to understand the pace necessary to complete a level, do two runs at the 1–10 time as part of your warm-up. This will show you the pace necessary to go out and come back in during the allotted time. Try to complete each run exactly on time. Try not to arrive too early for the PACED TIME or the RECOVERY TIME.

NOTE: Advanced 17- or 18-year-olds may reach a level as high as 22. Advanced 15-year-olds will probably reach up to level 16.

APPENDIX F: VERTICAL JUMP (ONE STEP)[*]

This is a fairly advanced test, probably not for use with players younger than 16. To record accurate measurements, coaches or trainers will need some sort of jump tester. Coaches on a budget may want to use something simple such as a Reach and Jump Board ($50). The U.S. Women's team uses a Vertec ($550), a device consisting of a metal pole and adjustable square vanes (or flags), to measure jump height.

Purpose

Some athletes may outwardly appear to be powerful and even score well when tested for vertical jump, but for some reason, not show this power on the playing field. These athletes may lack the deceleration ability, strength, coordination, flexibility, or some other variable which inhibits successful performance of a dynamic vertical jump. By allowing the athlete to take an approach step during the vertical jump test, we can determine the individual's ability to convert momentum from horizontal to vertical, which is thus a measure of transfer of power. The ability to out-head an opponent either defensively or offensively is an example of horizontal velocity, which must be converted to vertical lift.

Protocol

1. Stand under the Vertec. With the arm closest to the Vertec have the athlete "reach" high (with feet kept flat on ground) in an effort to touch and move the highest possible vane (or flag). This is the standing reach value.

2. The athlete takes a position an unspecified distance from the Vertec. (Hint: Find a comfortable starting point during practice.)

3. The athlete is allowed to take one full stride to a "plant" step (taking off with either

---

*From U.S. Women's Battery of Tests

one or two feet). This should place her in a position directly under the Vertec flags, thus maximizing potential vertical jump peak height.

4. During the jump, the athlete extends one arm as high as possible and taps the Vertec flags, pushing away the highest flag reached.

5. After a brief recovery, the athlete is allowed subsequent trials until she can no longer reach a flag.

6. The highest flag moved is recorded in inches.

7. The standing reach value is subtracted from the vertical jump score to determine absolute vertical jump. (Vertical Jump – Standing Reach = Vertical [one step] Jump Total.)

Resources

American Sport Education Program (ASEP)
1607 N. Market Street
P.O. Box 5076
Champaign, IL 61825-5076
(800) 747-5698
http://www.asep.com

American Youth Soccer Association (AYSO)
12501 S. Isis Ave.
Hawthorne, CA 90250
(800) 872-2976
(310) 643-6455
http://soccer.org

Fédération Internationale de Football Association (FIFA)
P.O. Box 85
8030 Zurich, Switzerland
011-411-384-9595
http://www.fifa.com

Human Kinetics
P.O. Box 5076
Champaign, IL 61825-5076
(800) 747-4457
http://www.humankinetics.com

Major Indoor Soccer League (MISL)
1175 Post Road East
Westport, CT 06880
(203) 222-4900
http://www.misl.net

Major League Soccer (MLS)
110 East 42nd Street, Suite 1000
10th Floor
New York, NY 10017
(212) 450-1200
http://web.mlsnet.com

National Alliance for Youth Sports
2050 Vista Parkway
West Palm Beach, FL 33411
(800) 729-2057
(561) 684-1141
http://www.nays.org

National Collegiate Athletic Association (NCAA)
700 W. Washington St.
P.O. Box 6222
Indianapolis, IN 46206-6222
(317) 917-6222
http://www.ncaa.org
http://www.ncaasports.com

National Federation of State High School Associations (NFHS)
P.O. Box 690
Indianapolis, IN 46206
(317) 972-6900
http://www.nfhs.org

National Soccer Coaches Association of America (NSCAA)
800 Ann Avenue
Kansas City, KS 66101
(800) 458-0678
(913) 362-1747
http://www.nscaa.com
Publishes *Soccer Journal* (print and online version)

National Soccer Hall of Fame
18 Stadium Circle
Oneonta, NY 13820
(607) 432-3351
http://www.soccerhall.org

**National Strength and
Conditioning Association**
1885 Bob Johnson Drive
Colorado Springs, CO 80906
(800) 815-6826
(719) 632-6722
http://www.nsca-lift.org

Positive Coaching Alliance
1001 N. Rengstorff Avenue
Mountain View, CA 94043
(866) 725-0024
(650) 725-0024
http://www.positivecoach.org

**Soccer Association for Youth
(SAY)**
4050 Executive Park Drive, Suite
100
Cincinnati, OH 45241
(800) 233-7291
http://www.saysoccer.com

Soccer in the Streets (SITS)
2323 Perimeter Park Drive NE
Atlanta, GA 30341
(678) 992-2113
http://www.sits.org

**United States Adult Soccer
Association (USASA)**
9152 Kent Avenue, Suite C-50
Lawrence, IN 46216
(317) 541-8564
http://www.usasa.com

United Soccer League (USL)
14497 North Dale Mabry
Highway
Suite 201
Tampa, FL 33618
(813) 963-3909
http://www.uslsoccer.com

US Club Soccer
716 8th Avenue North
Myrtle Beach, SC 29577
(843) 429-0006
http://www.usclubsoccer.org

U.S. Soccer Federation (USSF)
1801 South Prairie Avenue
Chicago, IL 60616
(312) 808-1300
http://www.ussoccer.com

**U.S. Youth Soccer Association
(USYSA)**
1717 Firman Drive, Suite 900
Richardson, TX 75081
(800) 4-SOCCER
(972) 235-4499
http://www.usyouthsoccer.org

MAGAZINES

Soccer America
P.O. Box 23704
1144 65th Street, Suite F
Oakland, CA 94623
(800) 997-6223
(510) 420-3640
 (20 issues/year)

World Soccer
King's Reach Tower
Stamford Street
London, England SE19LS
011-44-181-888-313-5528
http://www.worldsoccer.com

ADDITIONAL WEB SITES

http://www.goalie.com
http://www.pponline.co.uk
http://www.soccerconditioning.
    net
http://www.soccer-camps.com
http://www.soccerdrills.com
http://www.sport-fitness-advisor.
    com/soccertraining.html
http://www.soccerfitness.net
http://www.soccerpracticeplans.
    com
http://www.soccertv.com
http://www.topendsports.com
http://www.womensoccer.com

SUPPLIERS

Big Toe Sports
404 Holtzman Road
Madison, WI 53715
(800) 444-0365
http://www.bigtoe.com
(clothing, footwear, gear)

Eurosport
431 U.S. Highway 70A East
Hillsborough, NC 27278-9912
(800) 934-3876
http://www.soccer.com
(clothing, footwear, gear)

Reedswain
612 Pughtown Road
Spring City, PA 19475
(800) 331-5191
http://www.reedswain.com
(books, DVDs, equipment)

RefShop
Make The Call Athletics
1950 Bradley Estates Drive
Yuba City, CA 95993
(877) REF-S111
http://www.refshop.com

Soccer Learning Systems
P.O. Box 277
San Ramon, CA 94583
(800) 762-2376
http://www.soccervideos.com
(books, DVDs)

Soccer Master
14188 Manchester Road
Manchester, MO 63011
(800) 926-9287
http://www.soccermaster.com
(clothing, footwear, equipment)

Tru Mark Athletic Field Marker
P.O. Box 706
Norfolk, NE 68702-0706
(800) 553-MARK (6275)
http://www.athleticfieldmarker.com

Under Armour Performance Apparel
1010 Swan Creek Drive
Baltimore, MD 21226
(888) 7ARMOUR
http://www.underarmour.com

BIBLIOGRAPHY

Anderson, Bob. *Stretching: 20th Anniversary. Rev. ed.* Bolinas, CA: Shelter Publications, 2000.

Clark, Nancy. *Sports Nutrition Guidebook.* Champaign, IL: Human Kinetics, 2008.

Coaching Youth Soccer/American Sport Education Program. 4th ed., Champaign, IL: Human Kinetics, 2006.

DiCicco, Tony, Colleen Hacker, and Charles Salzberg. *Catch Them Being Good: Everything You Need to Know to Successfully Coach Girls.* New York: Penguin Books, 2002.

Foer, Franklin. *How Soccer Explains the World.* New York: Harper Collins, 2004.

Gardner, Paul. *Soccer Talk: Life under the Spell of the Round Ball.* Chicago: Masters Press, 1999.

Gifford, Clive. *Soccer: The Ultimate Guide to the Beautiful Game.* Boston: Kingfisher Publications, 2002.

Kirkendall, Donald T. *The Complete Guide to Soccer Fitness and Injury Prevention.* Chapel Hill: University of North Carolina Press, 2007.

Koger, Robert. *101 Great Youth Soccer Drills.* New York: McGraw-Hill, 2005.

Lauffer, Butch, and Sandy Davie. *Soccer for the First Time Coach.* New York: Sterling Publishing, 2006.

Muckian, Michael, with Dean Duerst. *The Complete Idiot's Guide to Coaching Youth Soccer.* Indianapolis, IN: Alpha Books, 2003.

Murray, Bill. *The World's Game: A History of Soccer.* Champaign: University of Illinois Press, 1996.

Price, Robert G. *The Ultimate Guide to Weight Training for Soccer.* Cleveland, OH: Price World Enterprises, 2003.

Provey, Joe. *The Confident Coach's Guide to Teaching Youth Soccer.* Guilford, CT: Lyons Press, 2006.

Radnedge, Keir, ed. *The Ultimate Encyclopedia of Soccer.* London: Carlton Books, 2003.

Siff, Mel. *Supertraining. 6th ed.* Denver, CO: Supertraining Institute, 2003.

Snyder, John. *Soccer's Most Wanted: The Top 10 Book of Clumsy Keepers, Clever Crosses, and Outlandish Oddities.* Washington, DC: Brassey's Inc, 2001.

Thompson, Jim. *Positive Coaching: Building Character and Self-Esteem through Sports.* Portola Valley, CA: Warde Publishers, 1995.

United States Soccer Federation and Michael Lewis. *Soccer for Dummies.* Foster City. CA: IDG Books Worldwide, 2000.

INDEX